BACKYARD STRUCTURES

AND HOW TO BUILD THEM

Monte Burch

THE LYONS PRESS
Guilford, Connecticut
An imprint of the The Globe Pequot Press

To buy books in quantity for corporate use
or incentives, call **(800) 962–0973, ext. 4551,**
or e-mail **premiums@GlobePequot.com.**

The Lyons Press is an imprint of The Globe Pequot Press.

10 9 8 7 6 5 4 3 2 1

Printed in the United States of America

ISBN 1-59228-010-2

Library of Congress Cataloging-in-Publication Data is available on file.

CONTENTS

INTRODUCTION

I like building things! It doesn't make a difference whether they are big, small, or in between. I like building furniture, sheds, outbuildings, and other structures. After living on our farm for more than 30 years I've put up a good number of outbuildings, poured dozens of floors, and constructed scores of other projects—including several hundred feet of stone walls and concrete walks. There have been several decks. (The first deteriorated because it wasn't constructed of the proper materials.) There have been numerous smaller projects including picnic tables, outdoor furniture, children's play yards, and several sandboxes. In fact, if archeologists dig through my backyard, they'll find a cache of Tonka trucks and cars.

With several books on the subjects, I've found many other folks have the same interest. It's fun, relaxing, and good healthy exercise to create projects for your backyard and home. And, of course, you add to its value. Today's new materials, tools, and even some new techniques have made constructing projects such as those in this book much easier. And, in most instances, they are of better quality and longer lasting than structures you could build just a decade or so ago. "Do-it-yourself" is booming, and one of the reasons is the ready availability of materials from the "big box" building supply houses. For instance, these days you can walk into one of those warehouse-style stores and find all the components you need for a deck, all in one spot. And many items make it simple and easy to build a deck, for instance, precut step stringers, precut balusters, pressure-treated materials for longer life, and composite materials that eliminate 99 percent of deck maintenance.

The projects in this book range from the simplest garden planter to a two-car garage/shop that does take a lot of hard work and some expertise in building framing. The book is divided into eight sections, with projects grouped in them. For instance, Section III is devoted to decks and patios, while Section VIII covers animal housing.

The number of folks interested in raising chickens may not be as great as those wishing to build a glamorous deck, but there are projects for all in this book.

I had a great deal of enjoyment in designing and constructing the projects in this book and hope you enjoy building them as well. Do make sure you follow all safety rules, and check with local building authorities as to code rules for your particular part of the country. These codes may vary greatly according to climate and geology.

Many thanks to Matt Weber of *Extreme How-To* for allowing me to use articles and photographs from the magazine in this book.

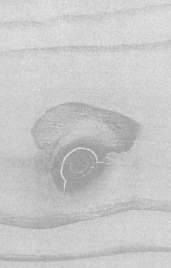

BUILDING IT YOURSELF—IT'S EASIER THAN YOU MIGHT THINK

Building your own backyard structures is easier than you might think. Even if you consider yourself all thumbs and have never before attempted a do-it-yourself project, there are a number of good "beginner" ones in this book. You can then work your way up to the most complex, such as building your own two-car garage/shop. Today's modern tools and materials also make it easier and less time consuming to build backyard structures—and often make them longer lasting.

CHAPTER 1

GETTING STARTED

WHERE TO BEGIN? Starting your first backyard structure may seem daunting at first, but if you divide a project into steps, it will seem easier.

PLANNING

The first step is to determine the kind and size of backyard structure you wish to build. If you decide to build a shed to hold garden equipment or other gear, make sure the shed is large enough to hold your equipment. Measure your lawn tractor or mower and any other equipment that will be stored in it. Make a scale drawing of the floor plan of the proposed building, as well as a scale drawing of the equipment. This is easily done using architectural scaled paper. Make sure the equipment will fit through the proposed door. Then measure your yard and, again using the scaled paper, create a "to-scale" yard or garden design that includes the structure or structures.

At this point you should contact local building authorities. Are there any rules, regulations or zoning ordinances that you must follow? Many municipalities regulate the size, type of construction, and spacing of structures from property boundaries and other buildings. You should also locate all utilities, such as underground cables, electrical service, plumbing, and sewer lines. Information on these is commonly available from building authorities, except in rural areas. In locating the buildings, make sure you do not build over any utilities.

When locating a structure, consider its planned use. For instance, shed doors are usually best facing the south, especially in areas with snow cover. Greenhouses must be

It's extremely important to properly plan backyard structures to match your existing buildings. The structure should also be properly designed for the purpose needed and to match existing topography as well as local building codes.

located to take advantage of full sun. This means they should also be on the south side of other buildings. If possible, shelters and play areas should be located in the shade.

You should also consider the topography and soil types, especially for buildings such as pole structures. Most structures do best on flat, well-drained land. If you do build on a slope, it will cost more for fill and construction. Pole structures do not do well on extremely sandy soils.

If not working from a drawing, make a floor plan and side- and end-view plan sketch of the building. These can not only be used to acquire permits, but they also give you a good idea of the details as you construct the building as well as make it much easier to order the required materials.

BUILDING PERMITS

Building permits are often required by municipalities or counties before construction of any permanent building. This ensures that the building adheres to local and sometimes regional building construction and zoning codes. These codes ensure your building is safe, inoffensive, and doesn't infringe on the rights of others. Building codes may determine whether a site is suitable, who can construct the building, as well as location in relation to other buildings, fences, and property lines. The type and use of the building, as well as general construction, are also normally dictated as well. For instance, footings and foundation depth and sizing may be specified according to local soil and frost conditions.

SAFETY

Building projects can pose dangers, both with hand and power tools. This is especially so with power tools. Power tools, even the less obvious ones, can injure you very easily and very quickly. The first rule is to stay alert. Don't work when you're overtired. Don't use power tools when under the influence of drugs or alcohol. Pay attention to what you're doing and keep children, visitors, and pets away from your work area, again especially when working with power tools.

The most important step in using a power tool is to read the instruction manual before operating the machine. Learn the machine's basic application, limitations, and specific hazards. Never use the machine in a dangerous environment. If used in a wet or damp location, or in the rain, shock or electrocution can occur. Keep the area around the tool free of obstacles. Make sure all machines are sharp, clean, and well maintained. Make sure all guards are kept in place and working properly. Remove all adjusting devices, keys, and wrenches, as well as scrap work pieces from the machine before starting. Use the right machine and accessories for the job for which they are intended. Use only an extension cord of good condition and recommended for the specific tool use. An undersized cord can cause loss of power and overheating. Make sure to secure the work piece, especially smaller pieces. Don't overreach—loss of balance can cause you to fall into a machine. Don't force the work piece through the machine. Never leave the machine running unattended. Always turn off the machine and unplug it before adding or removing accessories or adjusting or changing setups.

The dust generated from woods, wood products, and some other materials, including splinters, chips, and airborne debris, can be injurious to your health. Always operate machinery in well-ventilated areas, and provide for proper dust removal. Wear a

Building backyard structures can be fun and healthful exercise, as well as add to the value of your property. It's important to follow all safety rules, including those for specific tools, as per the manufacturer's instructions. (Photo courtesy Sears/Craftsman Tools)

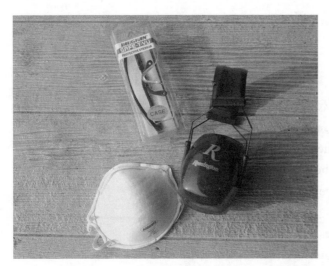

It's also important to wear the proper safety equipment, including hearing and eye protection as well as the appropriate dust or respirator mask.

dust or respirator mask if adequate dust and fume removal is not possible. Dust mask protection should comply with MSHA/NIOSH certified respirator standards.

Wear eye protection. Always wear safety glasses or a safety shield. Everyday eyeglasses are *not* safety glasses. Eye protection should comply with ANSI 787.1 standards. You should also wear hearing protection when using high-pitched power tools. Hearing protection should comply with ANSI S3.19 standards.

Wear proper apparel. Do not wear loose clothing, gloves, neckties, rings, bracelets, or other jewelry that may get caught in moving parts. Non-slip footwear is recommended. Wear protective hair covering if you have long hair.

Keep a first-aid kit on hand, as well as alcohol and tweezers for splinters.

Note: Your own skill levels should be taken into consideration when constructing the projects in this book. Neither the author nor the publisher can assume any responsibility for damage to persons or property resulting from the misuse of the information in this book.

CHAPTER 2

TOOLS YOU WILL NEED

OF COURSE, YOU'LL NEED tools to build backyard structures. The number and kind of tools depend on the scope of the projects you tackle and the amount of money you decide to spend. Good tools, however, are a very good investment. Buy quality and they will last not only your lifetime, but can last for several generations. I still have a number of tools from my dad, who was a contractor as well as cabinet and furniture maker. Many of those old, well-cared-for tools are as good as the day they were purchased. I also have several tools from my granddad and his brother, and they are also steadily put to use.

New tools, however, have an appeal of their own, and I can't resist hefting and admiring them. Many of the newer tools are much more user and ergonomically "friendly." If you don't already have the tools needed, you may wish to buy a few at a time as you tackle the different projects, gradually building on your knowledge and adding to your tool box.

HAND TOOLS

You can build any of the projects, even the most complicated in this book, with nothing more than hand tools. Hand tools are what my granddad and dad used to build houses, barns, and other projects. I've also used hand tools alone to build backcountry and farmstead buildings. The basic hand tools you will need include a hammer, handsaw, tape measure, square, and level, all of which can be simple, standard-sized tools.

Backyard projects can be constructed using hand tools alone. It does take more time, greater skills, and a bit more work. But traditional tools and traditional methods can still produce long-lasting, beautiful projects.

Modern-day innovations, however, make even the basic tools better, and you may wish to buy specific tools in sizes more suited to construction work than everyday repair, maintenance, and other chores. Let's start with the most important tools—hammers.

Hammers

Hammers are available in many sizes and shapes. The most common is a curved claw, 16-ounce hammer. It can be used for just about any home repair or maintenance work, cabinetry, millwork, and furniture building. A 20- to 24-ounce framing hammer is a necessity if you do extensive house framing. The larger hammer has a longer handle for better balance and force in driving large nails and is available with either a curved or straight (ripping) claw. The ripping claw can be used to pry up boards and pull up large nails. If you want the ultimate in hammers, the Ti-Tech Titanium hammer from Vaughn has interchangeable steel caps, and is ergonomically designed to combine the lighter weight of a titanium body with heat-treated high-carbon steel caps. A shingling hammer is handy for installing asphalt or composite shingles. The Vaughn 14-ounce Steel Shingling Hatchet has a 1¾-inch cutting edge for shingles and a retractable and replaceable blade for asphalt and composite shingles. It also has a 3-hole overlap gauge and a nail-pulling slot.

Always wear safety glasses when using hammers or other striking tools.

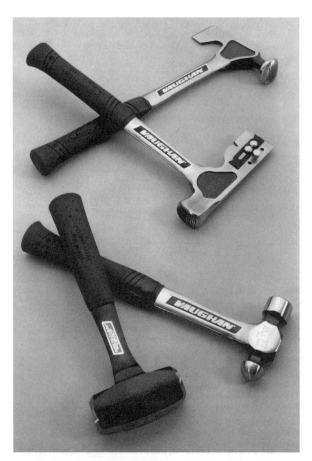

Hammers are extremely important. A 16-ounce hammer is fairly standard. The Ti-Tech from Vaughn has interchangeable steel caps. You'll also need heavy driving hammers for some chores, and a shingling hatchet is extremely handy for both composite and wood shingles, as well as for other chores. (Photo courtesy Vaughan & Bushnell Mfg.)

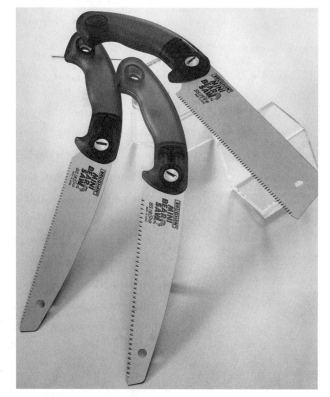

Handsaws

Next is a handsaw, and a standard length, coarse-cut saw with 8 points to the inch is a suitable choice for these projects. A hollow or taper ground saw is best for cutting treated lumber. A ripsaw can also be handy if you intend to rip boards for trim and other uses. If you're cutting heavy timbers, a timber saw, which features 3½ points to the inch, can be mighty handy.

A handsaw is a very important hand tool. A standard length, 8 point to the inch saw is a good choice. Fine-toothed saws, such as the Mini Bear from Vaughn, can be used for close-in trimming. (Photo courtesy Vaughan & Bushnell Mfg.)

Measuring tools, ranging from a small 16-foot to the longer 100-foot tape, are also needed. A carpenter's square, 45-degree square, and small pocket square can all be used for specific chores.

Measuring Tools

A 16-foot steel tape measure is a reliable all-around choice for most project work. The Stanley 16-foot Micro FatMax Tape Rule is reinforced with BladeArmor and features a patented 1¼-inch wide Mylar polyester film-wrapped steel blade, a patented end hook with wings for multi-catch, and grip versatility. For larger projects, a 50- or 100-foot tape can save time and ensure measurements that are more accurate. You will also need a square. A standard carpenter's square can be used, but a framing square is a better choice because it also has rafter framing tables imprinted on it. Both, however, are suitable for squaring boards for cuts and marking angles for rafters and other cuts. A smaller, aluminum tool pouch–sized combination square is handy for marking cuts on dimension lumber. This can also be used as a hand-held guide for cutting with a portable circular saw. Other squares that can be handy include a small adjustable square that has a 45-degree angle face. It can be used as a depth gauge, marking gauge, square, or angle square. A T-bevel is also extremely handy for marking precise angles.

Leveling Tools

You will also need a level and these are available in several sizes. A small, 2-foot level is adequate for some chores, such as laying concrete blocks, or for small projects. A 4-foot level is best for most construction projects. This provides a more precise reading for

Leveling tools are needed for some chores. These include handheld levels. The Craftsman SmartTool Plus Level offers a digital readout.

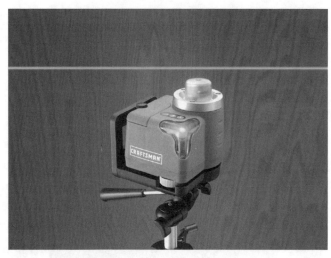

A plumb bob and string levels are also important for specific chores. Craftsman Rotary LaserTrac is great for laying out buildings. (Photo courtesy Sears/Craftsman Tools)

installing doors, windows, leveling, and plumbing framework. The Craftsman SmartTool Plus level provides angles by degrees and percent of slope or pitch in a digital readout. It also has acrylic level and plumb vials for quick reference as well. String levels are a good choice for laying out foundations, walls, or concrete floors. A plumb bob and string can provide precise location of building corners. The ultimate for larger buildings is a builder's or contractor's transit level.

Miscellaneous Hand Tools

A variety of miscellaneous hand tools can also be helpful, including a set of sawhorses. These can be handmade using sawhorse brackets or lightweight folding aluminum purchased horses. Ladders are also a necessity for many jobs. A small 7-foot stepladder and a 16-foot extension ladder will handle most chores.

Although most boring and many fastening chores these days are done by cordless drill/drivers, the "purist" can also do these chores with a brace and bit with a variety of bit sizes. The brace should be double acting, or able to rotate in either direction by turning a knurled knob.

Chisels and hand planes can be used for finish carpentry, smoothing, and fitting for precise joints. A No. 5

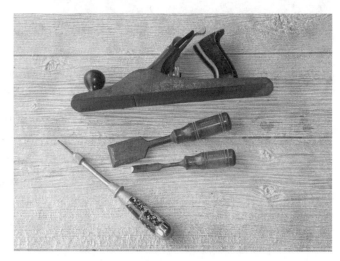

Chisels, hand planes, and hand drill drivers are other important hand tools.

The BowJak from Vaughan makes it easy to install twisted, warped decking boards. (Photo courtesy Vaughan & Bushnell Mfg.)

Portable power tools greatly speed up construction and are easy to use. They also allow many do-it-yourselfers to complete their projects with greater accuracy. The most popular power tool is a cordless drill/driver. These are available in several different sizes.

jackplane is a good all-around choice, while a set of four chisels, a ¼, ½, ¾, and 1 inch, will handle most cutting chores.

Installing decking boards can be a frustration with warped and crooked treated boards. The BowJak from Vaughn offers a quick and simple solution. The tool is tapped in next to the bowed boards and with the leverage of a pull handle, straightens the board before it is hammered in place. Straight blade and Phillips screwdrivers, as well as a variety of wrenches, are needed for many chores.

PORTABLE POWER TOOLS

Lightweight, portable power tools, especially cordless models, make many construction chores much easier, faster and, for most of us, more precise. Most portable tools are available these days as cordless. Cordless models feature battery power ranging from around 12 up to 24 volts. Drill/drivers, circular saws, saber saws, reciprocating saws, and even cordless compound slide saws all can be taken right to the job site, without the need for electricity. And, they're less cumbersome than corded models.

Cordless Drill/Driver

The single most popular portable power tool is a cordless drill/driver—and with good reason. These handy tools are one of the leading products sold in hardware and building supply stores, and the number one tool sold at Sears.

Choosing

First, decide how much voltage you need. The most popular models are the 12- and 14.4-volt models. Anything less than 12 volts can only be used for those occasional light drilling chores and for driving short fasteners into soft materials. Quality 12- through 14.4-volt models will handle most homeowner drilling and driving chores with care. For heavier duty, day-in-and-day-out usage, an 18-volt model is often chosen. These models can handle most fastening chores, even driving deck screws and metal fasteners fairly easily. For heavy-duty chores, the professional 24-volt models are hard to beat. They work especially well for around-the-farm or ranch chores and for heavy-duty tasks such as drilling in concrete or metal. There is, however, a price to pay. Not only is the cost of the tool higher, but the weight of the tool is also heavier as well. The 12- to 14-volt models are reasonably lightweight and easy to handle. The 18-volt models are quite a bit heavier, and the 24-volt models are heavy—some weighing as much as 3 or more pounds.

The next choice is whether to purchase a ⅜- or ½-inch drill. These numbers refer to the largest bit shank the chuck will accept. The most common is ⅜-inch. Many drill bits larger than that size are shouldered down to fit a ⅜-inch chuck. One-half inch chuck drills are normally higher priced, feature greater voltage, and are in the "professional" market.

Practically all cordless drills these days feature variable speed and reverse. Some of the better ones also feature two or even three variable speed ranges. The lower range is used for driving, the upper ranges for drilling. Most also feature an adjustable torque clutch, which is especially important for driving. It can be adjusted to allow the bit to slip at various torque settings, eliminating over-driving fasteners.

Keyless chucks have pretty well replaced keyed chucks on cordless drills, although they're still popular on many corded models. Keyless chucks are normally best for most woodworking chores, but they can slip on hard drilling/driving chores such as concrete or metal. One-handed keyless chucks are easier to operate than the two-hand versions, and they tend to have greater gripping power. The design of the chuck is important because of the way it's used. Normally you insert the bit, hold the chuck with one hand, and turn on the drill to tighten the chuck. A large knurled gripping ring is important because it allows for a better tightening grip.

The frustration of the short running times of past days has been alleviated by the introduction of high-capacity, nickel-cadmium or Ni-MH batteries. These can improve running time by as much as up to 30 percent over the old batteries. Drill/drivers are normally sold with a charger and a battery. Kits with two batteries, although more expensive, are best because you can keep one battery on the charger and one on the drill/driver for continuous use.

Many models also feature T-handles. These place your hand closer to the work for greater control and offer better balance and handling. Another feature to look for is an automatic brake that immediately slows down the drill when you release the trigger. High-end drills often feature bubble levels so you can drill or drive plumb or level, along with adjustable auxiliary handles for greater control and pressure on tough jobs. Ergonomics and soft-touch molded handles are common on newer models and drill/drivers do feel different. This is a case where you need to pick up several models at your local tool store to determine the model that best fits your hand.

An impact driver is best for heavier driving chores. It can be used with screws or to drive lag screws. Corded hammer drills can be used for boring in concrete and other extremely heavy-duty chores.

Everybody seems to sell these in a matching case, which is good for carrying them out of the store, but that's about all. Few serious do-it-yourselfers I know use the case because they keep a charger going with a battery in it at all times. The case is awkward to store, and only adds to the cost.

Using

The main reason for cordless drill/drivers, in addition to their convenience, is their versatility. Many drill/drivers come with a combination straight blade/Phillips driver in a snap-in stow for quick and easy accessibility. In addition to the normal drilling and driving operations, with a cordless drill/driver and a variety of accessories, you can do anything from mixing paint to wire-brushing scale from metal. You can also use hole saws for cutting holes for doorknobs and other chores. Grinders are also available for many different grinding operations. Polishers can make quick work of many cleaning and polishing chores.

The Milwaukee Sharp-Fire System utilizes a portable electric screwdriver with an extension and provision to hold a magazine of Sharp-Fire System Screws. Because you don't have to bend over to use the tool, it's ideal for decks, floors, and roofing.

Craftsman introduced one of the most innovative drill/driver products with their Speed-Lok Systems. Utilizing a Quick Connector fastened in the chuck, you can slide various bits or drivers in and out of your drill in seconds. This means you can drill a hole, slide out the bit, slide in the driver, and then drive the fastener, all in a matter of seconds. The connector and bits and drivers feature a hex end shank to prevent slipping, either in the chuck or in the connector. The main component is the Magnetic Screw Guide that features an open hex end into which hex drivers can quickly be slipped in or out to change from straight blade to Phillips in a variety of sizes. The outside sleeve of the guide also slides downward to hold the screw until it can be started. This is a great feature for driving long screws such as deck screws. A wide variety of bits and drivers are available in different Craftsman Speed-Lok kits.

Corded models do, however, offer greater power and there is not the problem of running out of energy with a low battery. Corded hammer-drills are particularly useful for heavy boring chores in concrete and other hard materials.

The Craftsman Speed-Lok System provides a number of easy-to-use quick-change drill/driver accessories, drivers, and bits. (Photo courtesy Sears/Craftsman Tools)

Circular Saws

Circular saws are actually the most important portable electric tools for fast and accurate construction of buildings and other larger projects.

Choosing

Circular saws are sized by the blade diameter the saw accepts. The size ranges from small 4-inch trim saws up to big 15-inch framing saws. Circular saws are available as corded or cordless, with the latter becoming increasingly more powerful and more popular. Corded saws are rated by horsepower and range from ½ up to almost 4 horsepower. A good all-around choice for most homeowner chores, and the most popular size available, is a 7½-inch saw with 2 to 3 horsepower. Cordless saws are rated by volts and range from 14 up to 24 volts. A good homeowner choice is an 18-volt, 6½-inch saw. Remember,

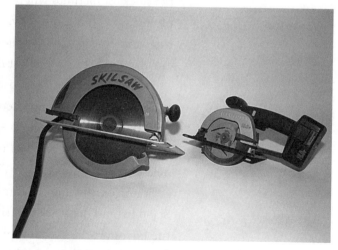

Circular saws are available corded or cordless and in a variety of sizes.

however, the deepest cut that can be made by a circular saw is just a bit less than half the diameter of the blade. This means a 6½-inch saw will easily cut through 1½- or 2-inch materials on a crosscut. The blade will cut through almost 3 inches of material, which will make a 45-degree bevel cut through 2x material. The larger the saw, the greater the power, but also the heavier the weight. The smaller trim saws are best for interior framing, even for cutting plywood or for chores where deep bevel cutting is not required.

Today's saws are extremely easy and comfortable to use with a number of great features. Black & Decker features a plastic window for easy viewing of the cut line in their cordless model. Skil's corded, 7¼-inch, 2.6 horsepower circular saw with Sight Light has a built-in light for better view of the work piece. The new Craftsman Laser Trac model features a laser light showing where the blade intersects the work piece. Makita's 7½-inch corded contractor saw comes with a carrying bag. Milwaukee's corded Tilt-Lok Handle Saw has an 8-position, user-adjustable main handle for maximum comfort and control in a variety of situations. A number of DeWalt corded saws feature an electric brake. Porter Cable offers a 4½-inch trim saw, and a 7¼-inch, 15-amp framer's saw with case. Several manufacturers offer cordless saws in a combo kit with a cordless drill including the Bosch and Craftsman 24-volt models and DeWalt, Milwaukee, Makita, and Grizzly 18-volt models.

Using

As with any power tool, safe usage of circular saws is extremely important. Make sure you follow all manufacturers' safety rules. Circular saws now feature a lockout button in addition to the switch and both must be pressed to start and run the saw. A spring driven retracting blade guard covers the blade except when pushed out of the way by the stock. Sometimes when ripping or making angled cuts, the guard must be manually pushed up and out of the way. A finger tab allows you to move the guard without getting your fingers close to the spinning blade. Always wear safety glasses when using a circular saw because sawdust can be thrown into your eyes.

The most common use of the portable circular saw is crosscutting stock. The stock must be well supported and preferably clamped on a sawhorse or work surface with the stock protruding well away from the edge of the support surface. In most instances, the line to be sawn is marked with a pencil and using a square or try-square held against the stock edge. The base plate of the saw has a line indicator. Position that indicator on the marked line, with the saw motor on the supported side of the stock. Stand behind the stock and slightly to the supported side. Align the line indicator with the line, start the saw, and push the saw into the stock. Use a steady, even motion to complete the cut. Be careful at the end of the cut that you don't angle off the line. You can also make the cut more precise by holding a try square against the edge of the stock

Next to cordless drills, circular saws are the next most popular portable electric tools.

with one hand and guiding the saw base plate against the square. The Craftsman Circular Guide Master allows you to make straight, angle, or bevel cuts quite easily.

Ripping is another common circular saw use and rip guides are standard with most of today's saws. Rip guides are fastened in the saw base plate with a thumbscrew and adjusted to the width of the stock to be cut. The guide is then placed on the outside of the stock, the blade started, and the saw pushed into the stock. Guide the saw with the rip guide riding along the outside edge of the stock.

Miter cuts can be made by first marking the miter lines with either a 45-degree arm of the try square or with a bevel gauge. In this case, you will have to lift the blade guard at the start of the cut.

Bevel cuts are made by loosening the angle adjustment knob and turning the saw to the correct bevel or angle. Compound miter cuts are made by setting the correct angle and then cutting at a miter as well.

Controlling the depth of cut is important. The depth of cut is adjusted by raising or lowering the saw base or saw blade. When cutting through heavy stock, make sure the blade is cutting full depth. When cutting thin stock, and especially plywood that may splinter fairly easily, set the blade to just barely cut through the material.

Rabbets can be cut in the edges of the stock by setting the saw blade to the proper depth and using the ripping guide to guide the blade. First, clamp a thick board to the stock to create a surface for the base to ride on and make the edge cut. Then remove the guide board and turn the stock down flat. Again, use the miter gauge to make the second cut to create the rabbet.

Dadoes can be cut by using a square clamped in place across the stock to guide the saw base. With the blade set to the correct dado depth, make the first outside cut. Then slide the square over to guide the saw for the second outside cut. You can then make the successive freehand cuts between the two outside cuts to complete the dado.

Plunge cutting or creating pocket cuts is also fairly easy with circular saws. Lay out the outline of the hole with a square and a pencil. Position the saw base front down on the wood surface with the blade directly over one line and at the rear of the cut to be made, but not touching the wood. Turn on the saw and, holding the blade guard up with the finger lever, slowly lower the saw into the stock until the base is flat on the wood surface. Continue the cut forward until you reach one corner. Repeat for the other cuts. Always turn the saw off and allow the blade to stop revolving before removing it from each cut. Do not try to back cut with the saw. Because of the curvature of the blade, a circular saw does not cut straight up and down and there will be a slight bit of stock left in all four corners. Finish cutting these with a handsaw or saber saw.

Cutting large sheets of plywood is fairly easy with a circular saw if you follow a few tips. First, make sure the large sheets are well supported. A pair of sawhorses is the initial start. Large, thin sheets, however, tend to sag. Use waste 2 × 4s between the sawhorses to support thin sheets. Snap a chalk line or use the Craftsman Accu-Rip circular saw guide to rip stock up to 24 inches in width. For crosscutting, set the saw blade to a depth just a little over the thickness of the plywood and cut across the waste 2 × 4s. Keep the 2 × 4s set aside for future plywood cutting chores.

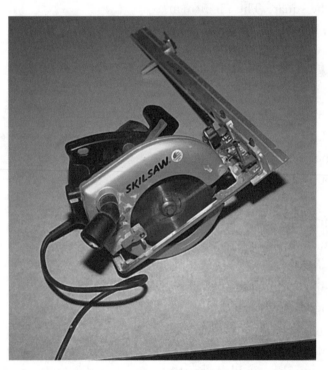

Large panels are easily ripped using the Craftsman Accu-Rip accessory guide.

A number of different woodworking blades are available for portable circular saws, including the standard general-purpose blades, rip, and cut-off, as well as smooth trim/finish, and even aluminum/laminate blades. Of course, there are also metal and masonry cut-off blades.

You can literally build a house with nothing more than a portable circular saw, hammer, measuring device, and square—and many carpenters have. Now you can even build that house without electric cords. But circular saws are even more versatile, depending on the saw or cutting blades used.

The Craftsman LaserTrac circular saw projects a bright laser line on the line to be cut. It's great for cutting off deck boards and ripping large panels.

Corded circular saws will also cut larger framing materials more easily. The Bosch lightweight CS20 models have a composite foot for lighter weight, and also feature detent systems, blowers, and rafter hooks. The detent system helps improve accuracy of cuts. An integrated powerful blower and patent-pending quadrant designed system quickly remove sawdust and ensures a clear line of sight. This provides an unobstructed sight line. The Craftsman LaserTrac saw projects a bright laser line directly on the line to be cut. This is especially handy when cutting large pieces of plywood because you can see the projected cut to the end of the panel, making it easier to produce a straight cut.

Reciprocating Saws

Reciprocating saws are also mighty handy for many backyard construction chores. Reciprocating saws have been traditionally thought of as contractor and remodelers' tools, but these days increasing numbers of homeowners are finding many uses for them. And, there are some jobs no other tool can do.

Reciprocating saws come with a variety of motor sizes, ranging from 7.5 amps up to 11.8 amps. Of course, the more powerful saws are also heavier. Most of the saws these days feature quick-change blade clamps that allow for quick and easy changing of the blades. Some also come with dual action. The reciprocating action is used for metal, while an orbital action can be more effective in wood. It's also important to note the

Reciprocating saws are extremely handy for many construction chores. Originally thought of as contractor tools, they're now popular with homeowners and do-it-yourselfers.

stroke length of the blade. Longer stroke lengths will cut more stock in a shorter time than will the shorter strokes lengths, and with less wear on the blade. In some instances of cutting in small places, however, the shorter stroke lengths may be necessary. Almost all of the quality saws on the market feature variable speeds. This allows you to adjust the cutting speed to the material. It also makes it easier to start the saw in many instances. Begin with a slow speed to get the cut started in the right location and then speed up to complete the cut.

Quite often reciprocating chores involve getting into tight spots. The Porter-Cable's Tiger Claw Variable Angle Saw combines two adjustable gear housings that allow the saw to be used in all kinds of cutting positions and conditions. The rear gear housing pivots 180 degrees up and down with 13 positive stops for close-quarters cutting. When locked at 90 degrees, the saw measures only 8½ inches. The blade housing also rotates 360 degrees with 12 positive stops. This allows you to configure the blade in any direction relative to the saw's body. It also features the Quick-Change blade clamp that allows you to make a blade change in less than 4 seconds without a wrench. The Porter-Cable Variable-Speed All-Purpose Tiger saw has both reciprocating and orbital actions.

The Milwaukee Hatchet reciprocating saw is a corded 7.5 amp model with an adjustable 6-position pivoting handle that is built for use in tight spaces. At only 6.7 pounds, this Sawzall reciprocating saw is easily maneuvered in tight spaces, such as under counters and between studs and joists. The saw has a steel connecting rod and steel gear that strengthens the saw and provides longer life. The saw is counterbalanced for less vibration and smooth operation. The tool cuts at up to 3,000 spm (strokes per minute) with its variable speed trigger. The saw has an orbital action that greatly enhances the speed of cut. The ¾-inch blade stroke length is ideal for close-quarter cutting.

DeWalt has a powerful, 11.8 amp saw providing a 1¼-inch stroke length and a variable speed dial system that allows you to dial in the exact speed you need. A counter balance and rubber grips provide more control and less vibration.

The Craftsman 8.5 amp Professional Reciprocating Saw has counter-weighted gearing to provide smooth operation with minimum vibration. Replaceable brushes help extend motor life. The saw has a 1⅛-inch blade stroke, tool-less blade changing and adjustable pivoting shoe that slides out for added control. The variable trigger allows no-load speeds from 0 to 2,600 spm. The ergonomically designed rear handle features a two-finger trigger for added efficiency and control. The saw comes with case and three assorted blades.

Black & Decker has designed a reciprocating saw just for the do-it-yourselfer. The saw is lightweight, weighing only 6.8 pounds, and is easy to maneuver in a variety of cutting conditions. A soft-grip rear handle and front boot add comfort and reduce vibration. The 7.5 amp motor provides variable speeds from 0 to 2,400 spm and also features Quick-Clamp tool free blade changes. It comes with a metal and wood cutting blade and case.

Hitachi offers an 11 amp saw with a unique swing action that cuts through wood material twice as fast as a conventional orbital action saw. It has a 1¼-inch stroke, a dial-in maximum speed elector, variable speed control switch, and a 1¾-inch keyless adjustable pivoting shoe.

To add even more versatility and a go-anywhere capability, reciprocating saws are also available as cordless models. This provides almost unlimited use on both wood and metal projects. Even with close-at-hand projects, you don't have a cord to mess with. The Black & Decker 18-volt Firestorm Cordless Cut Saw weighs only 6 pounds, 10 ounces, and is easy to maneuver into a variety of cutting positions. It features a variable-speed control trigger that controls the speed and a rotating shoe that fits tightly against cutting surfaces for accurate cuts. The 18-volt, high-capacity nickel cadmium battery delivers maximum power and run time. The 3,000 spm provide a fast cut and an electric brake stops the blade upon release of the trigger. The saw comes with a pruning attachment that stabilizes branches while they are being cut. The saw also comes in a soft bag for easy storage and portability. The multi-purpose bag has pockets for carrying other tools.

The Craftsman 19.2 volt Cordless Reciprocating Saw has a powerful 900 series, 4-pole motor with 1.4 amp-hour battery that delivers plenty of sustained cutting power. The battery charges to full capacity in 1 hour. Variable speeds range from 0 to 2,500 spm. The saw has a 1¾₆-inch blade stroke with tool-less blade change. An adjustable pivot shoe facilitates plunge cuts. A soft, over-molded front grip and rear handle add to operator comfort. It comes with one battery pack, a charger, two blades, and storage case.

The Makita 18-Volt MForce Reciprocating saw has tool-less blade changing, fast-stopping electric brake, tool-less shoe adjustment, and variable speed. The Bosch 18-volt model has dual cutting lengths, 1½-inch and ¾-inch stroke lengths. It also features tool-less changing and push-button foot adjustment.

The DeWalt 18-volt saw has a ⅞-inch stroke, 0 to 2,800 spm, and an electric brake that prevents blades from breaking when exiting a plunge cut. At 6.5 pounds, it's also extremely light. A pivoting shoe with open top provides maximum visibility and reverses for upside-down cutting. You can cut 50 2 × 4s, 144 1½-inch PVC pipes, or 30 6-inch roof vents on one charge.

Saber or jigsaws are useful for many chores, such as cutting holes in siding for windows and doors.

Saber/Jigsaws

Saber saws are just as handy. They can be used for cutting holes for windows and doors, for cutting electrical box openings, and for cutting round or irregular shapes. Saber saws are available in either cordless or corded models. The Bosch 18-volt saw offers a One-Touch Blade Change System, ejecting hot or broken blades with a touch of a lever. It features the patented Bosch Blade retention system: an exclusive three-way grip that maintains secure blade position for positive cuts. Bosch also has a Top Handle Orbital Jigsaw and a Barrel-Grip model. The latter makes it easier to do precise cutting. Porter-Cable has a heavy-duty corded Variable-Speed Quick-Change Bayonet saw with a 4-position orbital blade action. A dust blower keeps the line of sight clean. The Makita cordless 18 volt has tool-less blade changing, 3 orbital settings, and a blower that can be used as a blower or vacuum when attached. The Milwaukee corded T-Shank heavy-duty, fast cutting jigsaw features a powerful 6.2 amp motor, has Quik-Lok blade change system, and built-in dust collection port, as well as a full 1-inch orbital blade stroke.

STATIONARY POWER TOOLS

Stationary shop tools, such as radial-arm and table saws, along with drill presses, can be valuable for backyard construction projects. But, since they're in the shop, you have to tote the material to the tool. Portable "contractor" table saws, however, can be extremely useful, especially in constructing larger buildings. These are light enough to tote to the site, yet can be used for precise cutting.

Table Saws

Table saws come in several sizes and types. It's important to choose the saw based on your needs. The size of a table saw is rated by the blade size it will accommodate. Saws for do-it-yourselfers and contractors range from 9 up to 12 inches, but are available up to 24 inches for industrial use. A 10-inch saw is the most popular for most home shops and contractors. Table saws are also available in three basic styles. Small, bench-top models come without a stand and are often placed on a workbench. These saws are lighter in weight, so they can be moved around quite easily. Bench-top saws are suitable

Stationary power tools are extremely handy and accurate. They can do many chores, faster and easier than hand or portable power tools. They do, however, require shop or garage space.

The Craftsman Job Site saw is easily transported to the job on its own wheels with a retractable handle. (Photo courtesy Sears/Craftsman Tools)

for craft and hobbyist work. The next up in size are the contractor models. These are rugged and big enough to handle larger sheets of plywood and other materials, yet are lightweight and portable enough to be transported easily in the back of a truck. The Craftsman 10-inch Job Site Table Saw is designed to fold up and be transported easily and set up on site. A collapsible steel stand with 5-inch hard-rubber wheels and a retractable handle allows the portable saw to be transported like a rolling suitcase. The 10-inch Job Site Table Saw from Bosch comes with a folding steel stand and outfeed support. It's easily transported and set up on site.

Heavy-duty floor models, with a rugged stand and cast iron table, are the choice for the serious woodworking shop. These saws feature more precise fence control, usually larger table surfaces, and some are available with either 115- or 230-volt motors. These may be labeled "contractor" saws, but most are actually too heavy for easy transportation.

An excellent example of a quality do-it-all saw is the Delta 36–682–682KL Industrial 10-inch Contractor's model. The saw utilizes a $1\frac{1}{2}$ horsepower induction motor, 30-×-27-inch cast iron table with cast-iron extension wing and 30-inch Biesemeyer Commercial Fence System with 24-×-27-inch laminated table board. The latter system allows for precise cutting of larger panels, crosscutting longer pieces, and greater versatility for other operations. The table has "T" slots for the miter gauge and the extremely heavy-duty fence also extends well past the rear end of the table. This prevents any "turn-out" problems when stock is almost through the blade. All controls are easily worked and precise. The Auto-Set Miter Gauge has adjustable stops at 45 and 90 degrees. The see-through blade guard locks in the "up" position, and automatic insert release makes for easy and quick blade changing. The model also features a cast-iron carriage for minimal vibration and up-front, on/off paddle switch. The model has a maximum $3\frac{1}{2}$-inch cut capacity at 90 degrees and $2\frac{1}{2}$ inches at 45 degrees.

In a table saw, the blade stays stationary and the work piece is guided into the blade. The work piece is most commonly guided with either a rip fence or miter gauge. A sturdy, easily used, and precise rip fence is an important feature of higher quality saws.

For serious do-it-yourselfers, the Delta Industrial 10-inch Contractors' saw is an excellent choice. It comes with a cast-iron wing and a 30-inch Biesemeyer Commercial Fence System. It's extremely powerful, accurate, and easy-to-use.

For precise and easy use, the table saw must be set up properly. The fence must be precisely aligned with the saw blade. Today's table saws also come with a splitter and a blade guard. The splitter must also be aligned properly with the blade so the cut made in the work piece slides freely and the anti-kickback points must be properly working. Check to make sure the saw guard works up and down easily and is properly aligned with the blade. Table saws are fairly simple to operate. The only adjustments made once the saw is set up are raising and lowering the blade as needed, or tilting the blade for angle cuts. One accessory you may desire is a zero-clearance insert. This is especially important when cutting thin strips that may fall between the blade and the insert opening.

Miter Saws

Another extremely handy construction tool is a miter saw. These are light enough to be carried to the work site, yet like their bigger brother the radial-arm saw, provide a means to make fast, precise cross and angle cuts. Economical models are available to make only straight and angle cuts. Higher-end models feature a compound miter

Miter saws are light enough to be carried to the job site, but make quick and accurate work of cutting framing materials and inside trim. The Craftsman Portable Work Center holds the saw securely, adds versatility, and holds longer pieces for easy cutting.

setting. This allows for cutting compound miters on projects, such as crown molding. The Delta 12-inch ShopMaster Compound Miter Saw delivers maximum cutting power with its 15-amp, 120-volt motor that operates at 3,500 rpm with a 40-tooth carbide-tipped blade. It comes equipped with a tall sliding fence, extra large dust collection chute, extensions, and clamp.

One of the biggest problems with compound miter saws is visualizing the cut line. The Craftsman 10-inch arbor Laser Miter saw casts a laser light across the work piece to help provide a more accurate cut. The Porter-Cable 12-inch Twin Laser Compound miter saw has bright TwinLaser cut lines indicating both sides of the blade kerf, whether the blade is rotating or not.

Sliding compound miter saws utilize an arm for the saw to slide back and forth. This allows them to make cuts on wide-width materials. The Craftsman 12-inch model features a big, 20⅝-inch diameter worktable. The 10-inch slide Compound miter saw from Bosch has crown molding miter detents, 31.6-degree miter, and 33.9-degree bevel for quick, accurate cuts. Milwaukee 10-inch Magnum slide compound miter saw has an extra tall patented Flip Fence for either compound or miter cutting. A unique override mechanism allows fine adjustment near preset miter angles.

SPECIALTY TOOLS

A number of specialty tools can also aid in building backyard structures. Some can also provide for more precise cutting and fitting.

Air Compressors

An air compressor and mating air tools can do an amazing amount of work on backyard structures.

Choosing

Air compressors are available in a wide range of sizes, with different air delivery ratings, horsepower, and in single- and two-stage models. Single-stage models are the most common choices for home shop needs. It's extremely important to match the air compressor to the tool being used. All Campbell Hausfeld air compressors feature an air-delivery rating. This signifies a specific model's output power. To ensure proper performance from your air tools, use only those tools with air requirement ratings less than the delivery rate of your compressor. Campbell Hausfeld models are available in Standard Duty, Serious Duty, and Extreme Duty. The Standard Duty line is designed for occasional use in the home, garage, or workshop. Serious Duty is designed for more frequent use on the farm, automotive garage, or work site. Extreme Duty is for commercial work.

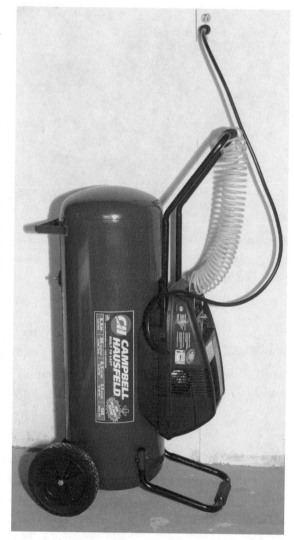

Air compressors are important and versatile tools. They're available in a variety of sizes.

Air compressors are also available in a range of sizes. Again, first choose the usage. Small portable compressors, including "pancake" styles, can run small tools around the house. Those with 2 horsepower can handle small jobs. Tank styles ranging from 5 up to over 6 horsepower can be used for almost any extreme how-to homeowner chore. The 6 horsepower models are about the limit in power for 120-volt, homeowner operation and are available with horizontal or vertical tanks. The new Campbell Hausfeld, 5.5 peak horsepower 22- and 26-gallon compressors are the only models on the market that can be stored and operated in either horizontal or vertical positions. "The 'vertizontal' design provides do-it-yourselfers with a great deal of versatility," said Brad Miller, Product Manager. "Users can choose compressor position based on preference or space allocation."

The Craftsman 150 PSI, li-free compressors use higher-pressure technology to pack more air power than any other single-stage units of their size. The compressors are

Any number of air tools can be used for backyard projects, including different types and sizes of air nailers.

equipped with high-flow regulators and push-to-connect couplers. Their commercial grade, electric motors have high-volume cooling fans and specially designed shrouds that direct the fan air for maximum cooling efficiency. For portability, the vertical and horizontal compressors are equipped with semi-pneumatic wheels and foam-grip handles.

Accessories and Tools

With just one compressor you can run an amazing variety of power tools. And even if used only for occasional homeowner repair chores, you'll get the job done more quickly and less expensively with air tools. In fact, Campbell Hausfeld offers more than 70 air tools.

Whether you are building a house, deck, gazebo, or a birdhouse, there's an air-nailing system to match the job. Campbell Hausfeld offers a wide variety of air nailers beginning with tiny ¼-inch crown staplers for finish carpentry and crafts. These tools are the choice when assembling drawers or craft projects such as bird and dollhouses. Moving up to the next size is a 1¼-inch brad nailer. Its primary use is installation of interior house trim, including baseboards. Brad nailers are also available in 2-inch sizes and are used in cabinet and furniture construction as well. Finish nailers are available in both 2- and 2½-inch sizes. These are also used in cabinetry and interior trim work. Craftsman has a 16-gauge finish nailer with 360-degree directional exhaust, and comes with ¼-inch nail stud. Next up in size are the 3½-inch clipped head framing nailers. These are used for house framing, sheathing, making trusses, and for decking. Craftsman offers a clipped-head and full-head, angle framing nailer. Both feature quick-release nosepieces for rapid removal of jams. The Craftsman clipped-head angle-framing nailer features a magnesium gun body for light weight and an inline magazine for better balance. It has a combination trigger, adjustable exhaust deflector, and an adjustable depth drive nosepiece.

The Porter-Cable 175 PSI High-Pressure Framing Nailer Combo Kit and associated compressor allow the nailer to weigh on average 25 percent less than other pneumatic framing nailers. This enables the user to use it longer without feeling fatigued. The nailer uses 32-degree, 2-inch to 3½-inch paper collated clipped-head framing nails. The nailer includes a tool-free magazine release for easy clearing of jams, a selectable trigger allowing the user to switch between restrictive or contact mode, a tool-free adjustable depth control, and a rubber grip.

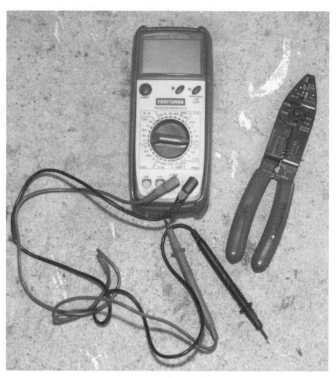

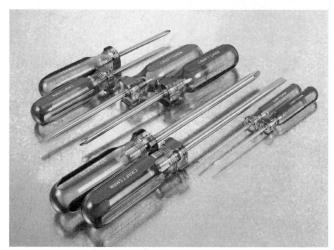

Specialty tools include tools for wiring, posthole diggers, shovels, plumbing tools, and lots of screwdrivers, pliers, and wrenches. (Photos courtesy Sears/Craftsman Tools)

Coil roofing nailers are used for asphalt and fiberglass roofing shingles, re-roofing, and sheathing. The RN175A Porter-Cable model also has a selectable trigger that works in either restrictive or contact mode. In addition, it utilizes a unique nail and drive system that incorporates a two-feed pawl system for reliability.

One of the more unusual nailers is the air palm hammer. This uses bulk nails and allows you to drive individual nails in tight areas for decks, fencing, and house framing such as joist hangers.

When choosing an air nailer, a rubber grip adds to the ease and comfort of use. Models with lightweight aluminum housings also add to the ease of use. A side-loading magazine is also easiest to load. Triggers may be sequential or single-cycle/contact, depending on the use. Dual-mode triggering with single-cycle/contact trip triggers allows you to easily switch between the two nailing modes. A contact-trip mode is designed for speedy operation with sheeting and other ready-to-nail materials. The single-cycle mode gives you better control and more accurate fastener placement when you have little margin for error. Those with an adjustable exhaust port allow you to direct the exhaust where you want it to go. Campbell Hausfeld sells these tools in kit form, which also includes the necessary accessories and a carrying case.

Other specialty tools may be required, depending on the types of jobs you tackle. If doing electrical wiring, you'll need pliers and screwdrivers with insulated handles, as well as electrical wire stripper pliers. Plumbing requires the use of a hacksaw. If doing copper plumbing you'll need a soldering set-up or a copper tubing cutter and flare making kit. Holes for posts and other projects will require digging tools, mattocks, shovels, and post-hole diggers.

CHAPTER 3

MATERIALS

A WIDE VARIETY OF materials may be used for constructing backyard structures. These materials include wood for framing and covering, metal or vinyl for covering, shingles for some roofs, composite materials for a variety of purposes, and a wide variety of fasteners.

WOOD

The choice of wood materials used for a backyard project depends mostly on whether the structure is enclosed and protected from the weather or exposed to it. Any materials exposed to the weather should either be naturally long lasting, insect, moisture, and rot resistant, or they should be treated to have these qualities.

One excellent wood choice is redwood because it has natural durability and resistance to insects and lasts longer outdoors than most other woods. Redwood is naturally a very stable and long-lasting wood. Redwood boards resist warping, cupping, splitting, and checking. Several different grades of redwood are available, with Construction Common and Deck Common suitable choices for most projects. If constructing in a damp area, use all-heart grades, Construction Heart, or Deck Heart. Redwood comes in two predominant colors: cinnamon-red and creamy yellow. The cinnamon-red color is heartwood and comes from the center of the tree. The creamy yellow wood is sapwood. When ordering redwood lumber, specify the intended use, grade, seasoning, size, and texture.

Many kinds of materials can be used for the various backyard projects, with wood the most common. (Photo courtesy Wolmanized Natural Select wood)

Outside projects require long-lasting, insect-resistant, and moisture-resistant woods. California redwood is an excellent choice for many backyard projects. It's beautiful, works easily, and is long lasting. (Photo courtesy California Redwood)

Another fairly common species of naturally long-lasting wood is white or western cedar. It is very easily worked, resistant to disease and insects, and has its own natural reddish golden beauty. Less common species include locust, cypress, and red cedar heartwood.

CCA-treated lumber has also been a tradition for outdoor construction, such as decks, playgrounds, play sets, and other outdoor use since the 1970s because of its resistance to termites and fungal decay. CCA contains copper, chromium, and arsenic. The Consumer Product Safety Commission, however, believes that hand-to-mouth behavior is a primary source of exposure to arsenic from CCA-treated wood play sets. Young children (generally children under 6 years of age) can then ingest the arsenic directly from their hands or indirectly when they touch food or toys, which are then placed in their mouths. Manufacturers of CCA-treated woods reached a voluntary agreement with the Environmental Protection Agency to end the manufacture of CCA-treated wood for most consumer applications by December 31, 2003, although CCA-treated wood will be available for some commercial applications. The EPA has indicated that some stocks of wood treated with CCA before this date might still be found until mid 2004. Treated wood has, however, not been banned.

According to Huck DeVenzio, from Arch Wood Protection, "The two prominent 'next generation' preservatives are copper azoles, used to produce Wolmanized Natural

Pressure-treated wood has been a popular outdoor building material for a number of years. The "next generation" of preservatives, such as those used to produce Wolmanized Natural Select wood, are much safer than the old chemicals. (Photo courtesy Wolmanized Natural Select wood)

Select wood and alkaline copper quaternary, used in wood sold under several brand names. The new copper-protected products look, last, and perform very much like the green-colored wood that has been in lumber outlets for decades." The patented preservative in Wolmanized Natural Select wood is a formulation of copper azoles. Copper, derived from recycled sources, is the principal ingredient, protecting against termites and fungal decay. Protection against copper-tolerant fungi is provided by organic azoles—Preventol, from Bayer Chemicals. Preventol is also used to protect many of the foods we eat such as fruit, peanuts, and wheat.

Softwood Dimension Materials

Enclosed projects or those with framing not exposed to weathering or ground contact can be constructed using standard softwood dimension lumber. This lumber is more economical than the woods suggested for exposed use. Dimension lumber comes in several grades, including Yard Grade No. 1, 2, 3, and 4 common, with No. 4 the most economical. The amount of knots, defects, and blemishes in the wood determines the grade. Select or structural-grade lumber is also available, including 1 and 2 clear, as well as C and D select. Clear denotes a board free of any imperfections. These are, naturally, much more expensive. In many instances, you may not find all the grades available at local suppliers. Kiln-dried

Lumber Dimensions in Inches

Nominal	Dry
1 × 6	¾ × 5½
1¼ (5/4) × 6	1 × 5½
2 × 2	1½ × 1½
2 × 4	1½ × 3½
2 × 6	1½ × 5½
2 × 8	1½ × 7½
2 × 10	1½ × 9¼
2 × 12	1½ × 11¼

Softwood dimension lumbers are commonly used for interior framing and interior projects. It's available in a wide variety of standard nominal sizes.

dimension lumber is available in several standard sizes 1 × 12s, 2 × 4s, 2 × 6s, 2 × 8s, 2 × 10s, and 2 × 12s. These are the nominal sizes. A 1 × 12 is actually ¾ × 11¼ inches. Boards are commonly available ranging in length from 8 to 20 feet.

Portable Sawmills and Green Woods

If you have the timber or trees, green woods can be cut and used for some backyard structures. This includes sheds and shelters, construction beams, and fencing. In the past, logs were dragged from the woodlot, hauled to a sawmill, and then sawed into useful sizes.

One answer for those with enough woodland is to use a portable bandsaw mill to saw logs into a variety of wood products. Portable bandsaw mills have been around for many years, but they have grown increasingly popular in recent years with numerous companies offering one-man or smaller models that are economical and easily transported into even fairly tight woodland areas. You can do less environmental damage in many instances by taking the mill to the tree, rather than dragging and hauling the log to the mill. Most companies also offer the bigger, commercial mills as well.

These portable bandsaw mills offer many advantages to those willing to spend a little time and hard work in their timberlands. First, even pole or small diameter timber can be milled into posts and beams for post and beam construction. Or beautiful woods, such as walnut, can be cut into turning blocks. Not all trees grow straight and

Rough-sawn wood, slabs, and green woods can also be used for "rustic"-type projects. Small-sized portable bandsaw mills, such as the TimberKing model shown, can be transported right to the tree.

perfect, and suitable for saw logs. Even walnut, one of the most desired woods, may grow into a gnarly, twisted tree if not given proper care. Commercial loggers rarely use these types of trees because the saw log lengths are not feasible for use on commercial saw logs. Years ago I used a bandsaw mill to cut a big old gnarly walnut into 2½-inch slabs. I even used the crotch and knot areas. Now I have about 30 possible rifle stocks along with I don't know how many shotgun stocks and pistol grips of beautifully figured walnut, air-dried in my barn and ready to work up. Several hundred dollars was realized from one single, usually wasted tree.

Of course, sawing lumber into planks is the main use of sawmills. These planks can range from as thin as ¼ inch up to whatever thickness you desire. Another advantage of bandsaw mills is they make a very thin cut, so little wood is wasted, even from small logs. And, the cut is very smooth. If building rough-sawn buildings, steps, decks, outbuildings, or other construction projects for your backyard, no further smoothing is required. Sawmilling with a bandsaw mill becomes quite addictive, especially on the figured woods such as walnut. As the planks are cut and the grain is revealed, it's like opening a Christmas present. You never know what will be revealed.

With a large bandsaw blade rotating around covered wheels, bandsaw mills are much less dangerous than circular mills. And, they're less intimidating and easier to use than circular mills.

The TimberKing 1220 mill is an excellent example of a portable, "personal" bandsaw mill. It will handle logs up to 29 inches in diameter and is a compact, affordable mill. Woodlot owners who want to mill their own select trees use these handy little mills. They are also popular with woodworkers who want better control over the quality and price of their lumber; by farmers and ranchers who always need boards and timbers for barns, equipment sheds, corrals, and fencing; by hunters and anglers who want to build or improve a camp or cabin; and by homesteaders who want to build their own homes, barns, and outbuildings. The TimberKing 1220 has heavy-duty spring-loaded loading ramps, a massive welded steel cutting deck, 4-position log stops, 6 leveling feet, and comes with a 15 horsepower, electric-start Kohler engine. An optional transport package takes the mill right to the trees and features 12-inch highway wheels, 4 sidewinder jacks, tongue, and complete light kit.

Milling Steps

The procedures used in sawmilling are fairly easy with units such as the TimberKing. The log is rolled up onto the cutting deck using a cant hook and the spring-loaded ramps. Large logs may require more than one person to safely and easily move them up into position, at least for the first cut. A cant hook easily turns even larger logs for succeeding cuts. Lumber is sawn either plain-sawn or quarter-sawn. Quarter-sawn is primarily used by woodworkers to create beautiful and unusual grain patterns. Plain sawn,

These mills can be used to saw lumber for many types of projects.

creating "common" grade lumber, is the most common method. The log is basically first sawn on all four sides to create a square "cant." Once the log is in position, it is dogged down using the dogs on the platform. The mill is started up and a slab cut from the top. The log is then turned 90 degrees, dogged in place, and a second slab removed. The log is again turned 90 degrees, slabbed, turned again, and slabbed. The resulting cant is then ready to be sawn into planks of the desired thickness, all with straight edges and ready to use for rough projects. The log is then simply sawn into planks of the desired thickness.

Curing

Wood that is to be used for rough projects, such as out-buildings, fences, cabin steps, and decks, can be used as soon as it is cut. It is best, however, to air-dry most lumber for a month or so in a well-ventilated building and out of the sun. Hot sun allows the wood to dry ex-tremely quickly and can cause checking and cracking. This isn't as much of a problem with timbers for timber framing or logs for creating log buildings as it is with thinner planks.

Woods to be used for woodworking or finer home construction projects must be dried down to around 6 to 8 percent moisture, measured with a moisture meter. The traditional method for home-millers has been to air-dry.

In most cases, sawn woods should first be air-dried before using for construction.

A surface planer/molder, such as the Woodmaster shown, will allow you to create your own lumber for backyard projects.

Air-drying lumber is an age-old method that requires nothing more than a barn or other dry storage space and plenty of time. The soft woods, such as pine, will dry in a couple of years. Hardwoods, such as oak, hickory, and walnut, may require up to 10 years, depending on the wood, plank thickness, and drying conditions. Even at that, you'll experience some "waste" from end splits, checking, and even warping unless properly laid for drying. The drying stack must be well supported up off the ground. Before stacking, coat each end with boiled linseed oil or paraffin. Place a layer of planks on the supports, making sure they're supported at least every foot, and that all boards are perfectly flat. Place ½- to ¾-inch wood stickers spaced about 1 foot apart on the just-laid planks. Add another layer of planks over the stickers, and then add more stickers and layers until you complete a stack. Make sure the top stack of boards is well weighed down so they won't warp upwards. Some air-dryers like to cover the stack with a plastic drop cloth for a month or so to prevent excessively fast initial drying.

A variety of small home-drying kilns are also available that can be used to dry the wood more consistently and at a much faster rate. It only takes a few months for even most hardwoods. Plans for creating your own drying kilns are available from the Department of Forest Products, Virginia Polytechnic Institute and State University Extension. For more information check out the Web site: www.woodweb.com.

SIDING MATERIALS

Many different types of purchased siding materials are available for backyard structures including solid wood, plywood, wood-based components, such as hardboard or oriented strand board, metal, such as aluminum or steel, and vinyl. Each type has its advantages and disadvantages. You may wish, however, to match the structure siding to your house décor and siding.

Solid wood is the traditional siding material, and in many cases, it's still preferred for its natural beauty. Next to masonry, it is the highest in cost, mostly due to the availability. It, however, is a renewable resource, whereas some products require non-renewable materials, such as petroleum, to produce. The type of wood chosen is extremely important. Wood decays and attracts wood pests and can also mildew and mold. The more

A variety of siding materials may be used for projects, including many solid wood products. Even better is engineered wood such as SmartLap Treated Engineered Wood Siding from Louisiana-Pacific. (Photo courtesy Louisiana-Pacific)

economical woods are the pines, but they are also the shortest lived. Some woods are more resistant, but also more expensive. These include redwood and white cedar siding, as well as cedar shake shingles. In addition to the traditional shingle, clapboard, and board and batten, new styles are also available including half-log styles that can turn your home into a "log" home. In most instances, solid wood siding is painted or stained and requires repainting and staining on a regular basis, the timing dependent on location and climate. Some homeowners, however, prefer to leave solid woods such as cedar shake shingles to weather naturally. Preservative-impregnated shingles can also be used in climates where mold and mildew are a problem.

Exterior plywood is a strong, relatively inexpensive siding. Available in 4-×-8 and 4-×-10 foot sizes, it's easy to install and goes on fairly fast. Sheets are normally installed vertically. Plywood comes as a flat sheet or with grooves cut in a pattern. Several different grades are available with the better grades having few patches. Plywood requires paint or stain on a regular basis.

One of the most versatile and economical sidings is hardboard. This manufactured wood product consists of wood fibers held together with a resin that bonds it all under heat and pressure. Hardboard is available in individual pieces resembling clapboard or in panels either applied vertically or horizontally, and with a wide variety of textures. A resin coat and a factory-applied primer protect the surface, but in many cases it must be

Exterior plywood is a popular and easy-to-use siding product.

painted. Hardboard is less durable than plywood and is prone to rot, chip, and break, especially if it's not installed properly to seal and protect it from moisture.

Oriented strand board or OSB is created in the same manner, except the strands are all oriented in layers that are again impregnated with resin and cured with heat and pressure. SmartPanel and SmartLap, treated engineered wood sidings from Louisiana Pacific, have the look of real wood, but with engineered strength. They are treated against fungal decay and wood-destroying insects. The next generation SmartSide siding and exterior trim products from Louisiana Pacific are treated engineered wood products designed to combat the damage caused by termites and fungal decay. These products are treated with SmartGuard process, which incorporates a borate-based additive that is fused throughout the engineered wood and protects the siding and trim.

Metal sidings consist of aluminum and steel, shaped to resemble solid wood siding. Once the popular alternative to wood, aluminum siding has pretty well ceded in popularity to vinyl, except in the Eastern states. Aluminum siding is low maintenance, durable, won't rot or corrode and pests can't damage it. Installation is similar

Hardboard, in a variety of textures, colors and thicknesses, is also a popular and economical siding material.

to vinyl. Aluminum siding has either a smooth or wood-textured surface that is factory coated. As the color applied is a top coat, it can be scratched and does fade. Aluminum can buckle in heat if not applied correctly and can also be dented.

Steel "lap-style" siding resembles aluminum in appearance, but is stronger and less likely to buckle or dent. It's a popular siding in areas where hailstorms are prevalent.

Steel panels are very popular siding and roofing materials for sheds and other shelters. Used on pole buildings, barns, outbuildings, and even framed sheds and other buildings, the covering goes on fast and is fairly economical. Steel panels are available in several different patterns, in plain galvanized as well as in a wide variety of colors. Unless insulated, a steel panel building tends to condense and sweat on the inside. Steel panels can also be dented by hail and will rust if scratched.

Metal sidings are often used for barns and outbuildings. It's economical, easy to install, and long lasting.

Vinyl is the top-selling home siding material these days and it does have several advantages. First is cost. Vinyl siding is relatively inexpensive compared to some other sidings. But the real reason for the increasing popularity of vinyl is the minimum

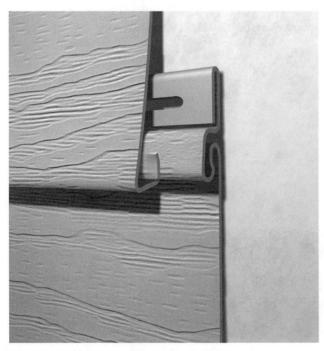

Vinyl siding is the top-selling home siding and if you're matching an existing side of your home, the choice for outbuildings. (Photo courtesy Louisiana-Pacific)

Soffit material as well as door, window, and corner trim is all available to match or contrast with vinyl siding. (Photo courtesy Louisiana-Pacific)

upkeep. Vinyl eliminates the need to repaint. Merely washing it occasionally is all the maintenance normally needed. Vinyl does have the advantage over metal in that the color is mixed in the material as it is extruded, so the coloring goes all the way through. Scratching doesn't bother it. Vinyl is impervious to insects and won't peel, flake, or blister. Another reason for the popularity of vinyl is the increasing variety of "designer" colors and styles available. Most vinyl siding is molded to resemble horizontal siding in the four most common forms, wide and narrow straight-edged clapboard, Dutch or shiplap, and beaded edge. Vinyl siding is also available in vertical styles to resemble board and batten, as well as cedar shakes.

ROOFING MATERIALS

Metal panels are also extremely popular as roofing materials. Again, they're quick and relatively easy to install, are economical, and come in a variety of colors. They are also very popular for pole buildings.

Asphalt or composite shingles are the choice in many full-framed sheds and buildings, especially if matching existing building roofing materials. They do require a wood decking to be installed first, followed by a layer of roofing felt, and finally the shingles. These types of shingles come in several different durability levels, based on their warranty, called 20-year, 30-year, and even 40-year shingles. Today, composite shingles are not only available in a wide variety of colors, but also different styles. Some even resemble shake shingle designs. Shingles are sold in a bundle, enough to cover one third of a square. A square is 100 square foot, or a 10-✕-10 foot area, or a combination

Metal panels are also common for roofing. In the past they've primarily been used for outbuildings, but newer, better-looking products are fast becoming popular with homeowners as well.

Composite shingles are traditional and still provide an economical, long-lasting roofing material and are easy to apply.

of measurements to reach the 100-square foot figure. Of course this type of roof is quieter in rainstorms, provides a certain amount of insulation, and doesn't create condensation beneath it. It is, however, more expensive than metal panels.

FIBERGLASS MATERIALS

Greenhouses, carports, and patio and deck covers are often constructed of plastic or vinyl panels. The Suntuf panels are made of polycarbonate and are virtually unbreakable. They block 100 percent of the harmful UV rays and they are available in 8 colors and 5 light transmission levels. Accessories mated to the materials make them easy to install.

COMPOSITE PRODUCTS

With the look of wood, but more durable and with almost no maintenance required, composite decking, siding, and other products have become increasingly popular for many backyard structures. Although resistant to termites and rot without harmful chemicals, these products are, however, a great deal more costly. Louisiana-Pacific Corporation's WeatherBest composite decking has a natural wood look and can be used for deck and dock surfaces, porches, walkways, and around pools. It is manufactured with a proprietary process that produces random but directional graining. Depending on the way the planks face the light, individual planks can appear slightly lighter or darker than surrounding planks. Just as with exotic woods, WeatherBest planks can have some subtle color variations from plank to plank, even with the grain

Composite materials are available for decking, house siding, and accessories. They are extremely durable, and apply just like their wood counterparts. (Photo courtesy Louisiana-Pacific WeatherBest)

going all in the same direction. This results in a rich wood character that is hard to distinguish from wood decking.

WeatherBest products are made of recycled wood fibers and "high-density" polyethylene plastic, providing it with added strength and durability (some composites on the market use "low-density" polyethylene plastic.) It cuts, drills, and installs like wood, but is never twisted or crooked like wood, nor will it rot or decay like wood.

A constant deck-owner complaint is the time and money required to maintain a deck. Composite decking, such as WeatherBest, is much easier and less expensive to maintain than a traditional deck. It needs no year in and year out staining or protective coating, and there is no need to annually replace rotting or splitting boards. All you do is power-wash it twice a year. WeatherBest composite decking comes in Premium and Select with matching railing, fascia, and trim components. The WeatherBest Premium line features exclusive reversible boards with random embossed graining patterns on one side and a rough-sawn texture on the other to provide the utmost in design versatility. It comes in three rich colors: driftwood gray, pacific cedar, and western redwood. The Select line comes in rough-sawn pine and rough-sawn gray.

FASTENERS

The correct fasteners must also be used for the different projects. Fasteners exposed to the weather, such as those on decks and other projects, should be coated with a protective coating, or be made of brass or stainless steel. Stainless steel fasteners are the ultimate, but are fairly expensive. Brass doesn't corrode with most woods, but doesn't have as much strength as some other materials. Fastener coatings include galvanizing, anodizing, and zinc plating. Galvanized fasteners are the least expensive and most commonly used. They will corrode with some treated woods and tend to stain cedar and redwood. Stanley-Bostitch has introduced THICKCOAT galvanization, a new line of fasteners specifically designed to protect against today's more corrosive pressure-treated lumber with Alkaline Copper Quaternary (ACQ). This new fastener-coating technology uses an enhanced electrogalvanization process to apply more than 2½ times the amount of zinc than conventional electroplating, and couples a chromate layer to each nail for exceptional rust resistance. THICKCOAT Galvanized Fasteners are available in a wide variety of wire-weld collated stick and coil-framing sizes.

Anodized fasteners are coated similar to galvanized fasteners and cost about the same. Zinc-plated fasteners are similar, but higher in cost and hard to find. Exterior screws, such as the Phillips brand for decks and other projects, are often coated with a ceramic or other mechanical type of coating. They do not stain or corrode any of the woods and are readily available at building supply centers.

Nails are available in a wide variety of types and sizes including general-use nails, pole-construction nails, metal roof nails, asphalt shingle nails, siding nails, and duplex head nails for use in constructing concrete forms. Nails are sized according to their length and the gauge of the wire used in construction. The most commonly used general-purpose nails include No. 4, 6, 8, 10, and 16d. Nails are also available as common, box, casing, finish, and brad, depending on the head design. Common and box are used for framing, casing, and finishing for trim work and brads for light-duty chores.

All fasteners exposed to the weather must be weather resistant, galvanized, zinc-coated brass or stainless steel.

These days, with the power of cordless drill/drivers, my favorite fasteners for many outdoor projects are the self-starting exterior wood screws such as the Phillips brand. Available in coated, brass, or stainless steel, they're quick and easy to use and extremely strong and durable. The newer composite decks require different types of fasteners. The FasTen MasTer TrapEase composite wood deck screws eliminate mushrooming in all leading brands of composite decking.

Metal fastening plates are also available in a wide variety of shapes and sizes. The various wood components are anchored together by nailing the plates to them. The most common include joist supports, truss plates and mending plates, angle clips, framing anchors, splicer plates, rafter ties, straps, corner reinforcements, heavy-duty L's, and heavy-duty T's. A number of DeckTie Connectors provide a complete connector system for deck construction. These include the Deck Board Tie, a handy system that eliminates hammer dents and has no visible nails for a clear hardwood-floor appearance. There are no rust stains on the surface, no countersinking, and no water puddling on nail heads.

FINISHES

The natural color and beauty of solid woods, such as redwood, is often heightened by simply applying a clear water-repellent finish with a mildewicide. Or you can bleach and use a weathering stain to produce a driftwood gray effect. Semi-transparent stains and solid-color stains or paints may also be used. Make sure the finishes are specified for exterior use. The composite wood products require no finish; the other woods require a renewed water-repellent coating every few years.

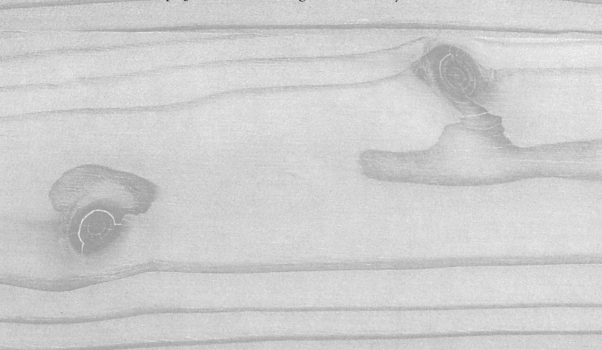

SECTION II

MASONRY PROJECTS

Masonry such as concrete and stone can be used for any number of backyard structures, including retaining walls, patios, walks, flowerbeds, and more. Masonry is fairly easily learned, although in some instances it does require a few specialized tools. Masonry is hard work but also a lot of fun and good exercise. And you can create a stone or concrete project that has a lasting sense of solidity.

CHAPTER 1

WORKING WITH CONCRETE

CONCRETE IS ONE OF the most versatile
building materials. It can be used for anything from entire buildings to portions of buildings, sidewalks, patios,
postholes, steps, and even decorative projects. Concrete
work is easily learned, although it can be backbreaking.

TOOLS

The tools needed for concrete work include woodworking tools for building forms. A hammer, hand crosscut
saw, portable circular saw, measuring tape, square, level
and string level, along with a small sledge and a maul, are
required for building the forms. A pry bar is needed for
disassembling the forms. A builder's transit or a laser level
can make it easy to level or place a form to grade.

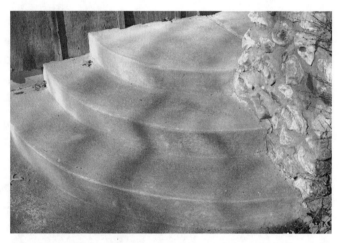

*Concrete is one of the most versatile building materials. It can be formed
into almost any shape imaginable, is strong, and has many decorative uses.*

Concrete preparation tools are also required. The tools needed depend on the jobs you
will be doing. Shovels and hoes are required for moving the liquid concrete around.
Rubber knee-high boots are needed for wading in the wet concrete. For small jobs, a
wheelbarrow or mixing box is required for mixing the materials. A mortar hoe with
holes in it makes it easier to mix the materials. A power mixer can also be mighty handy
for even small- to medium-sized jobs.

    Concrete finishing tools include a screeding board that is longer than the pour
to pull the concrete off and level it with the form edges. A tamper can also be helpful

Specific tools are needed for finishing concrete. The Marshalltown Apprentice Tool Kit has all you'll need in a convenient canvas carry bag. Tools feature DuraSoft handles for easy handling.

in settling concrete in the forms. Other essential finishing tools include: an edger, groover, magnesium or wooden float, finishing trowel, pointing trowel, cement broom, and a water hose. For larger projects such as floors or slabs, you'll need a bull float with a bracket. The Marshalltown models include their Auto-Just or RotaLeveler. Marshalltown also makes it easy for the beginner with a Concrete Apprentice Tool Kit. It includes: finishing trowel with DuraSoft handle, magnesium float with DuraSoft handle, wood float, groover, curved end edger, margin trowel, and Marshalltown "Tips" book, all stowed in a sturdy canvas tool bag. For large projects, you may wish to rent a power trowel. The materials in concrete can irritate the skin, so wear long-sleeved shirts, pants, and gloves.

MATERIALS

Concrete is a mixture of sand, gravel, and Portland cement (this is not a brand name, but a type). Cement is available in five types, but Type I, which is carried by most building supply dealers, is the most commonly used type for homeowner projects. The materials must be mixed with enough water to form a semi-fluid state that is then poured into a form. Concrete is heavy and the single key to safe and effective pours of concrete is building sturdy forms. Concrete is available in three ways: individual bags of cement, normally packaged in 1-cubic foot bags of 94 pounds, which is mixed with separate gravel and sand aggregates; QUICKRETE, which comes in a bag, prepackaged with the required aggregates; and ready-mix, which is delivered by a truck to the site. QUICKRETE offers the most convenience for small projects, such as anchoring posts. Merely mix with water according to the package information and pour in place. Mixing your own with cement and aggregates is more economical, but you must have the separate materials on hand and measure them properly. This is also a good choice for small- to medium-size projects. Mixing with a powered cement mixer should be considered for medium-size projects. With this method you can, for instance, pour a wide walk in sections, forming one section, pouring it, allowing it to cure, and then pouring another. For strength and performance, concrete pours should be done all at one time, unless they're fairly large, in which case they're poured in sections. The cement, sand, coarse aggregate, and water must be mixed in the correct proportions in order to create a durable, long-lasting job. There should be enough large aggregates (gravel) to make the mix economical, yet there should be enough small aggregates to fill in the spaces around the larger ones. There should be enough cement to hold all the materials together and there should be the right proportion of water to mix the materials and bind them together. The amount of water needed varies with the dampness of the sand. The less water used, the stronger the concrete, but there should be enough water to make the material workable. A fairly common mixture for foundations and footings is 1 part cement, 3 parts small aggregates, and 4 parts large aggregates. Driveways, garage floors, walks, and steps should be mixed 1 part cement, 2 parts small aggregates, and 3 parts large aggregate. I like to mix with a square cement shovel. Merely count the shovels of each of the materials. You can also use a bucket as a measuring device. The amount of water for average work, with slightly damp sand, which is fairly common, is about 6 gallons of water per bag of cement. Finer pours, for basement walls, walks, garage floors, and driveways, with the same moderately damp sand would require about 5½ to 5¾ gallons of water. However much water you are using, thoroughly mix the dry materials together first, then slowly add the water, thoroughly mixing as you go. You may find you don't need quite as much water, or you may need more.

If building a floor, slab, or foundation, the best choice is ready-mixed delivery. To order the correct amount of concrete tell the supplier the width, length, and thickness of the slab or foundation you intend to pour. They'll help you calculate the quantity needed. On smaller jobs you can calculate your own. The following chart from Marshalltown provides the basic information on cubic yards required:

Area in Square Feet (width × length)	10	25	50	100	200	300
4-in. thick	0.12	0.31	0.62	1.23	2.47	3.7
5-in. thick	0.15	0.39	0.77	1.54	3.09	4.63
6-in. thick	0.19	0.46	0.93	1.85	3.7	5.56

(Cubic yards do not allow for losses due to uneven subgrade, spillage, etc. Add 5 to 10 percent for such contingencies.)

FORMING

If forming a sidewalk or slab the first step is to dig up the area and remove all sod and debris. The area should also be recessed the depth desired. For instance, a 4-inch pour might be recessed so the top is slightly above ground level. The entire area should be well compacted and of a uniform depth. Keep the ground slightly moist as well. Construct the form using 2 × 6s, then drive stakes into the ground on the back side of the forms about every 3 to 4 feet apart. Drive or cut off the stakes flush with the tops of the form boards. Fasten the stakes to the form boards using duplex nails, or those with double heads so they can be pulled out after the concrete sets up. Curved areas can be formed with ¼-inch plywood or hardboard. Make sure the forms are level or of the grade desired. A carpenter's level can be used for small projects, a string level can be

The first step in creating a concrete project is building a form to hold the semi-liquid material in place until it sets up. Good, solid forms are a must because concrete is extremely heavy. Shown are batter boards used with string to lay out a slab for a garage floor.

Duplex nails are used to fasten form boards together. Their double heads allow for easier dismantling of the form once the pour has been made and the concrete set up.

Forms must be leveled or to grade. Craftsman Smart Tool electronic angle finder displays digital angle, level, or plumb. It has an audio tone that beeps at level and plumb. It also displays each angle in degrees or percent of slope.

A string level is invaluable. The Craftsman Line and Surface Level set comes with a standard line level and a pitch line level. The latter indicates the degree of pitch for establishing drainage on patios, walks, and so forth.

Builders and contractors often use a transit to establish grade and construct forms. Transits range from a few hundred dollars to over a thousand.

used for long runs, but a builder's transit is best for larger pours. Establish a uniform grade, using sand or fine gravel 1 or 1½ inches deep. If the slab is large, you will need to divide it into smaller, easily worked sections. Driveways and garage floors will need to be reinforced with steel rods or wire mesh. Footings and foundations should also be reinforced according to local code regulations. Driveways and garage floors are usually poured 4 to 6 inches thick. Sidewalks and other works are usually poured 3 to 4 inches thick. Foundations and footings are poured to code.

A completed garage floor form. Note the pour is on a slope and the interior has been filled with a rock-dirt fill. A layer of gravel will then be installed and steel reinforcing added before the pour.

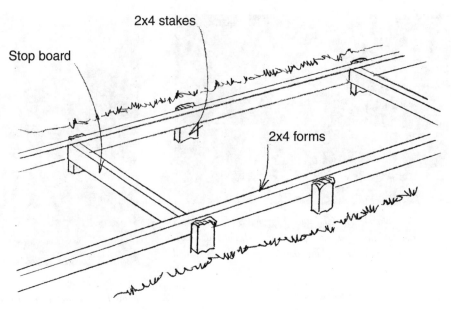

A concrete walk is one of the simplest projects and a good "beginner" project. Shown is typical forming before the gravel or sand base.

MAKING THE POUR

Concrete should not be poured on extremely hot, dry days because the concrete will dry out before it can cure properly. Concrete should also not be overworked. For this reason, the concrete should be spread evenly and quickly once the pour begins. Make

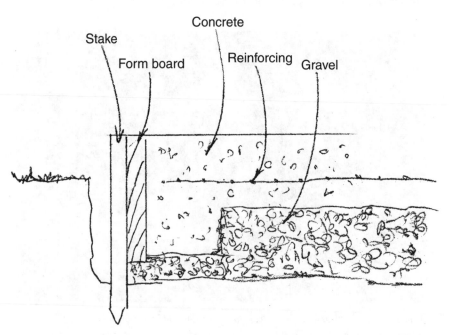

A driveway or patio may have a stiffener edge to add strength. Note the use of gravel and steel reinforcing materials.

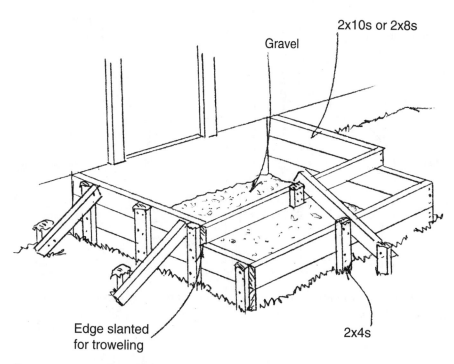

Concrete steps are another common concrete project.

sure to overfill the forms slightly. If the pour is overworked, too much water will be floated to the surface, which can cause scaling after the concrete dries.

Once the concrete is well spread over the area and into all corners and crevices, use a screed board to drag off the excess. This is a two-man operation and at best is hard work, especially on larger pours. The screed board should extend past the form edges about 3 inches on either side. Beginning on one end of the form, place the screed board over the form boards and then, using a side-to-side motion and at the same time pulling the board, inch it across the form boards to the opposite end. Screeding levels

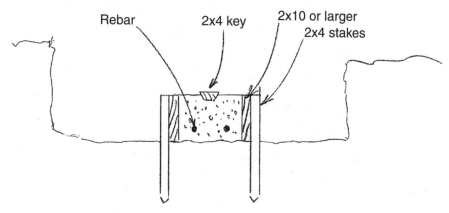

Concrete footings and foundations for buildings are fairly complicated chores, both in building the forms and in making the pour. Footings must follow regional guidelines as to frost depth.

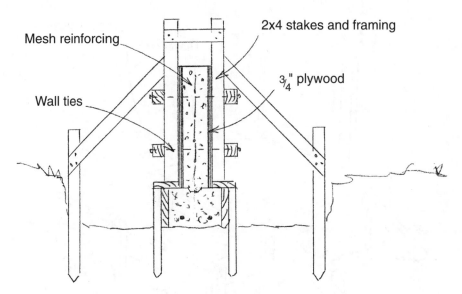

Mesh reinforcing

2x4 stakes and framing

Wall ties

3/4" plywood

House foundations and basement walls require expertise and specialized equipment. The inexperienced should leave these jobs to the pros.

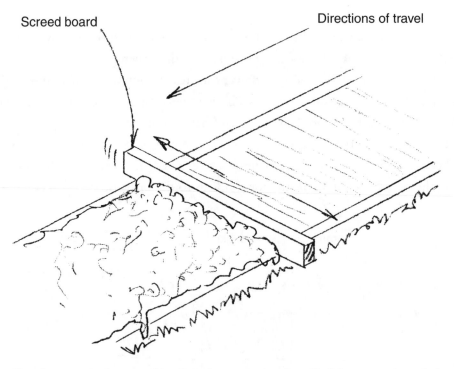

Screed board

Directions of travel

Once the concrete has been poured in a form, the next step is to "screed" off the excess and smooth the material with the top edges of the form. The board is pulled against the concrete and worked side to side at the same time.

A wooden or magnesium float is then used to smooth up the concrete and work the aggregate down.

the concrete with the tops of the form boards, pulling off excess concrete. Any low spots will be visible and should be immediately filled and the area rescreeded.

The next step is to float the surface. Small projects can be floated with a wooden or magnesium float. This helps fill any small voids and works the aggregate slightly below the surface. On larger pours, a bull float is used. The float is pushed away from you across the surface with the front edge slightly raised to prevent the blade from digging in. Then the float is pulled back at an almost flat angle. The Marshalltown RotaLeveler bull float bracket allows for easy changing of the float level on the push and pull strokes. Floating smoothes the surface and works some water to the surface.

A bull float is used on larger pours.

FINISHING

Concrete finishing consists of several steps. Concrete finishing results in either a roughened or a smooth surface and some of the steps should be done regardless of the desired roughness of the surface. The first step is to use a pointing or margin trowel to separate the edge of the concrete from the form. Then use an edger around the top edge of the form. This creates a rounded edge that won't chip off when the form is removed. The edger should be held fairly flat, but keep the front tilted up slightly when moving forward and the rear tilted up slightly when moving backward.

Jointing is the next step on projects such as sidewalks and driveways. This prevents the slabs from cracking. Control joints are normally spaced at intervals equal to the width of the pour. It is recommended, however, not to exceed 10 feet in any direction without a joint. The joint should be cut at least a quarter of the depth of the slab and a jointer tool is used for this step. Place a straightedge across the surface and run the jointer along the straight edge to create a nice straight line. As with the edger, hold the front up slightly when pushing forward. Control joints

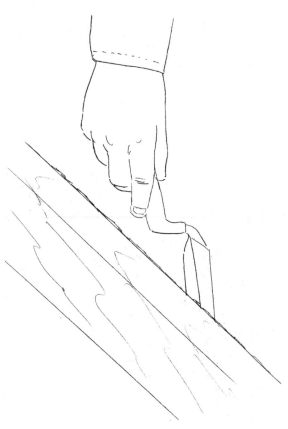

A pointing trowel is used to "cut" the concrete edge away from the form board.

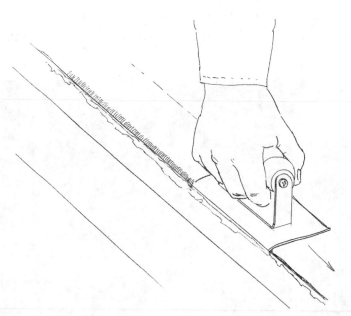

An edger is then used to slightly round the edge of the concrete and prevent it from breaking when the form boards are pulled away.

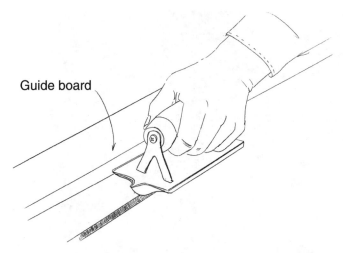

Guide board

Grooves must be cut in larger slabs. A groover held against a straight edge such as a 1 x 4 or 2 x 4 produces a nice straight line groove.

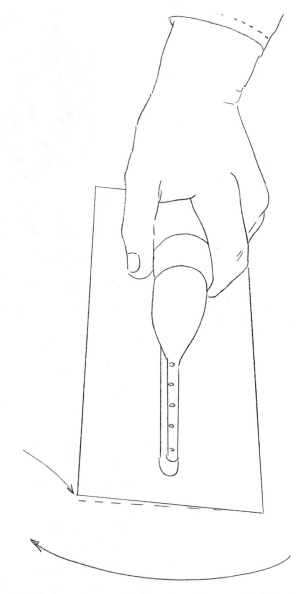

The final step is to smooth the surface using a trowel. A hand trowel can be used for small chores. The trowel is worked in an arc. The trowel edge, in the direction of the arc, is held up slightly and the "back" edge pressed down to produce a smooth finish.

in large slabs can also be cut after the concrete cures by using a masonry blade in a circular saw or concrete saw.

A float is used next to smooth and level the surface. This will also help remove any marks left by the edger or jointer. For rough or textured surfaces, use a wooden float. For projects requiring a smoother finish, use a magnesium or aluminum float. Hold the float flat on the surface and move it in an arc, overlapping the arcs as you proceed. Don't overwork the surface.

The final finishing step is troweling. Small projects can be hand troweled. Marshalltown recommends a 14 × 4 or 16 × 4 trowel for most finishing jobs. The first troweling should be done with the blade held flat down on the surface. Again, use the trowel in an arc, overlapping each previous arc by about a half inch. The surface should be well troweled several times to produce a hard, durable surface. Allow the concrete to set up slightly for the additional trowelings. The proper time is when the sheen of water disappears and a footprint leaves an indent shallower than ¼ inch. These trowelings should be done fairly vigorously and with the trowel tilted up slightly, pressing down with the edge. A power trowel is the best choice for large slabs. These units can be rented at tool rental shops. Troweling will provide a smooth, hard, and slick surface. These surfaces are easy to clean, but can be slippery when wet. Lightly brooming the surface with a shop broom after troweling can provide a rougher, more non–slip surface.

You can also rent a power trowel for finishing large surfaces.

CURING

Keep the concrete damp for five to seven days after pouring. Do not allow the concrete to dry out. Cover it with plastic sheeting and dampen the surface down every day or so.

Creating a "Brick" or "Country Stone" Project

One fun and unusual project is using concrete in special forms to create walks, patios, and courtyards. The QUICKRETE WalkMaker form is available in brick or stone patterns and they also have cement colors in brown, buff, red, and charcoal to make the projects look more natural.

Place the WalkMaker level on the ground. (You may prefer to remove the turf first.) Mix the color with the water and then add it to QUICKRETE Fiber-Reinforced Concrete according to the instructions on the package. Do this in a mixing tub or wheelbarrow. Fill the mold cavities with concrete. Smooth the surface on all edges with a pointing trowel until even.

Immediately remove the mold and move it adjacent to the section just completed. Repeat the process until the project is done. Keep the surface damp for about 7 days to allow the concrete to cure properly. After the entire project has cured for a week, sweep QUICKRETE Mortar or Sand Mix between the bricks or stones. Make sure the materials are well packed down in the crevices, and then hose off the excess.

You can turn almost any humdrum concrete project, such as a patio, into an exciting decorative addition to your home using Bon Tool Company Bon Way Decorative Concrete Systems. [Photo courtesy Bon Tool Company]

TEXTURED CONCRETE

Texturing concrete to resemble masonry materials using BonWay Tool texture mats is a very interesting project. A Plain-Jane concrete patio immediately takes on the appearance of anything from ashlar cut stone to London cobblestone or old Mexico tiles. The steps are simple. Finish the concrete in the conventional method. Add Bon True Color Hardener or Bon Ironex Integral Colors to the concrete, (the latter is added directly to the concrete during mixing), and then apply Bon True Color Release agent. Before the concrete sets up, tamp texture mats in place. Wash off any excess release agent with a pressure washer. Finally, apply Bon BossGloss or Boss Matte Clear Enhancer. *Voila!*—an exciting new patio or walk.

CONCRETE REPAIRS

Contraction and expansion due to hot and cold temperature variations or ice and frost can damage concrete, creating cracks and breaks. These days concrete repair is fairly simple due to a

The system uses Bon's texture mats and concrete colors to simulate ashlar cut stone, London cobblestone, random stone, Old Mexico tile, and other stone effects. [Photo courtesy Bon Tool Company]

wide range of modern adhesive compounds. The most common is latex cement. Two agents are blended together to create a quick hardening solution. Vinyl patch repair requires only to be mixed with water. Epoxy concrete repair comes in a kit with an emulsion, hardener, and cement. When all three are mixed according to the instructions, the material is virtually impregnable and will bond to just about anything, including steel.

Whichever material is used, it's extremely important to clean all dust, dirt, and loose materials from the area. Driving a few masonry nails into the area can provide "anchors" to help hold the material in place. Then mix the materials according to the package instructions. Apply and trowel smooth.

SAFETY TIPS

Concrete materials are heavy. Prevent back injuries when lifting bags by squatting and using your legs—not your back. Wear goggles to prevent eye injuries from splashing materials. Use a dust mask to filter out concrete dust. Wear waterproof shoes to protect your feet if standing in concrete. Wear rubber gloves to avoid skin irritation. Wear kneepads when floating or troweling.

CHAPTER 2

WORKING WITH STONE

THE AGE-OLD CRAFT of stonework is very satisfying. A stone project has a sense of timelessness. Many stone buildings, walls, walks, and fences are centuries old. You can use stone around your own home to build long-lasting and beautiful projects such as patios, a garden walk, steps, a retaining wall, flowerbeds, or even a building, if you have the patience and desire. Stone also blends in with almost any décor, from traditional to formal to rustic. Although the basic stonework used for these types of projects is fairly simple, the chore of working with stone is not easy. In fact, it can be backbreaking work. It's important not to lift more than you can carry, and use your entire body, not your back when lifting. It's also important to not try to do too much in a day's time, especially if you're not accustomed to heavy work.

Many old-time stone projects were made from stone picked up from fields, hillsides, or creek beds by the builder or property owner. Most homeowners these days, however, will have to purchase stone for their projects. Several different types of stone are available including granite, limestone, marble, slate, flagstone, sandstone, gneiss, and tap rock. Stone is also available as either fieldstone, rubble stone, or quarried stone. Fieldstone consists of rocks in their natural shape, and the wide variety of shapes and colors can add to the design of informal stone projects.

Quarried stone is cut and shaped and is used in more formal projects. Cut stone is slabbed at the quarry, but the face is left natural. A good example is slate or flagstone for patios or walks. Rubble stone are the pieces left over from blasting and cutting the cut stone. Ashlar stone pieces are cut on all 4 sides to create a formal pattern. The face

Stone is the ideal building materials for many backyard structures. It is available in a wide variety of colors, types, and shapes.

of ashlar is also cut or faceted in a decorative manner. This is the type of stone seen on churches and many commercial buildings. Naturally, the most expensive stone is ashlar, quarried stone the next, and fieldstone and rubble the most economical.

Because of the cost of shipping, the choices of stone may be limited in some areas. It's wise to visit local stone yards before you plan a project to determine the choices available. Stone is sold by the cubic yard. To figure the amount of stone you will need, calculate the cubic volume in feet by multiplying the length times the width

A wide variety of projects can be constructed using stone.

Stone projects can include patios, walls, and steps.

times the height. Then divide the cubic feet in the project by 27 to determine the cubic yards needed. If purchasing cut stone, add 10 percent for breakage and waste. With rubble stone, which is not graded but is purchased in bulk, you will need 25 percent more. In most instances, the stones will be delivered to your site. If transporting them yourself, do not overload your vehicle.

Whether you are building a wall, patio, or walk, pick stones that have flat, fairly square sides. Round or cannon ball stones are hard to work with—they don't stay in place dry-laid and are difficult to secure even with mortar. Once you have the stones delivered, sort them into piles of different sizes, shapes, and colors. This will make designing your project easier.

Stonework requires only a few tools. You'll need heavy leather gloves, goggles, a tape measure, a sharp bladed trowel, brick or stonemason's hammer, and a chisel. For mortared projects, a wheelbarrow, mortar shovel, and hoe, or powered mixer are also required. For flat projects such as walks and patios, you'll need stakes and string. To build stone walls, you'll also need stakes, string, a level, and a plumb bob.

Stone is laid dry or mortared. Following are a few sample projects.

DRY-LAID STONE GARDEN WALK

This is one of the easiest stonework projects. The walk can be created with cut stones for a formal pattern or with fieldstone for an informal look. Two methods are used. The first method is to cut the turf to the shape of individual stones, digging the soil down to level the stones and positioning them level with each other. The second method is to outline the walk with stakes and string, cut away the sod, place pressure-treated 2 × 4s or landscaping timbers on either side and place the stones down flat with the side timbers. Then fill in around the stones with sand.

DRY-LAID STONE PATIO

A dry-laid patio is created in the same method as a dry-laid walk. In this case, the patio is outlined with stakes and string, the turf removed, and the area excavated to the depth of the stones, plus 2 inches. Again wooden sides are used to outline the patio. Place a 2-inch layer of sand in the bottom and then rake the sand flat and smooth. Use a raking board to even out the sand and make sure it doesn't have any high or low spots. The sand should be somewhat higher in the middle or next to a building to create water drainage. After the sand has been leveled, sprinkle it with water to pack it down and provide a more solid surface.

Position the stones in place, with about 1-inch spacing around the stones. Make sure they are set level, don't wobble, and are of an even height. Once all stones have

The first step in constructing a dry-laid patio or walk is to lay the stones in position and then dig a shallow depression to seat them.

been positioned, sprinkle sand between the joints, making sure all joints are well filled. Then spray the patio lightly with a hose on mist to dampen the sand. Wait a bit and add more sand to areas that are low. Spray again to settle the sand and then lightly sweep away the excess.

MORTARED STONE PATIO

A formal, mortared stone patio consists of first a concrete pad to support the stones. The flagstone or slate pieces are then placed in a bed of mortar and mortar placed in the cracks. The excess mortar is cleaned away before the mortar has a chance to set. This is a more complicated project requiring concrete as well as stonework skills.

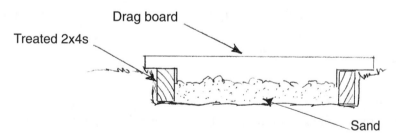

Walks and patios can also be constructed on a bed of sand. Treated 2 x 4s can be used to outline the project and a drag board used to level the sand.

The sand is then dampened and the stones laid in place and sand swept into the cracks between the stones.

DRY-LAID STONE WALL OR FENCE

Another fairly simple project is a dry-laid stone wall or fence. A dry-laid stone wall makes a fairly good low-height retaining wall because the open areas allow water to run through without building up pressure behind the wall. A dry-laid wall can be laid out to follow the contours of the garden, in a straight line, a squared shape, or curved. The number one rule? Do not build a top-heavy wall that is dangerous. A good mason's rule of thumb is a wall up to 3 feet in height should be at least 2 feet in thickness. For each additional 6 inches of height, the wall width must be increased 4 inches. Low-height walls are usually created with plumb faces. Higher walls must be constructed with a taper to the top. Generally, this is about one-fifth narrower than the width of the wall base. Walls higher than 3 feet must have a footing that extends below frost line. Even with low walls, you should remove the turf, and good stonemasons usually lay the bottom course below ground level. Because dry-laid walls are simply held in placed by the weight of the stones, it's important to choose fairly flat, thin stones. Avoid round stones.

The first step is to outline the wall inside and out using stakes and a string line. A top and bottom string line should be placed on the stakes. This provides a means of keeping the wall face plumb if desired. Lay the bottom layer of stones against the inside and outside string line. Normally a stone wall or fence consists of two outer stones with filler stones in between. Continue laying the next course, making sure to overlap the face sides of the wall. About every 4 to 6 horizontal feet install a "bond" stone. This stone should overlap from front to back of both faces and tie the faces together. Close off the open end of the wall with 3 large stones to create a U shape. The most important factor is to make sure the stones overlap and all are stable, with no rocking or loose-fitting stones.

MORTARED STONE WALL

A mortared stone wall has a more formal look, even when fieldstone is used. It is also a great deal more work, and the work goes slowly because you can only mortar a single course or layer at a time. A mortared wall can, however, be made from less select stones. Its appearance can be varied with a variety of shapes, types, and colors—and even colored

For mortared projects, such as a wall, mortar is mixed in a wheelbarrow using a mortar hoe.

mortar. Keep in mind though, a mortared wall is a permanent structure. If you don't like it, you'll need a sledgehammer to take it apart.

Construction is quite similar to a dry-laid wall. The main difference is the mortared wall must have a footing 4 to 6 inches wider than the wall and extending below frostline. The footing should be placed a couple of inches below the turf and then the soil graded back up to the wall.

String lines are used to outline the wall and a layer of mortar troweled in place.

Again, stakes and string lines are used. One method is to place a bottom string line just about an inch below the approximate height of the first course. Simply move the string line up as you lay additional courses.

The next step is to mix the mortar. Use a mortar mix of 1 part Portland cement to about 4 parts sand, plus a little water. Add a little bit of lime to make the mortar stickier. Don't get the mortar too wet or it will not support the weight of the stones. Add water a bit at a time. Stick your trowel down into the mixed mortar. The trowel should stand upright and not slump down. If it slumps, add more cement. A mortar batch that is too dry, on the other hand, sets too quickly to allow for easy masonry work, so never mix too much mortar at one time. Laying stones is slow work, and a large batch of mortar may dry before you can use all of it.

Place a layer of mortar under the string line and extending into the wall the approximate thickness of your largest stones. Place the first course in the mortar, scraping away the excess mortar squeezed out. Place a first course on the back side of the wall in the same manner. Place rubble rocks between the two courses, flinging mortar in and around the rubble rocks to hold them in place. Allow this course to set about an hour. Then remove excess mortar in the joints between the rocks. The mortar should be somewhat set, but not solid. Use the end of a round-headed bolt to scrape the mortar out of the joints and create a "sculpted" look to the wall. Use a hand broom to whisk away loose mortar and then use a steel brush to remove mortar from the rock faces. Allow the first course to set overnight.

When building a mortared wall, stones are laid with an outside and inside layer, or course.

Thin stones are used as face stones. They are propped in place until the mortar sets.

Now you're ready to lay the second course and it is done in the exact same manner. Place a layer of mortar; add the inner and outer face stones. Fill with rubble and add mortar in the center of the wall. Like a dry-laid wall, bonding stones reaching from front to back should also be placed about every 4 to 6 feet. It's a good idea to build up each corner or end first, then build between them. Use the old mason's rule of overlapping stones for strength: two stones go over one; one stone goes over two. There should

Rubble stones are used to fill out the center of the wall.

Mortar is applied over the rubble stones. Normally, only one course of stones is laid at a time.

never be a vertical joint of masonry between the stones. In some instances you may need to prop up some stones with wooden sticks, until the mortar sets.

A partially mortared wall has the appearance of a dry-laid wall, but is held more securely with mortar on the inside. The mortar is kept at least 4 to 6 inches away from the face of the stones.

Before the mortar sets completely, excess mortar is removed with a round bolt head and a whiskbroom.

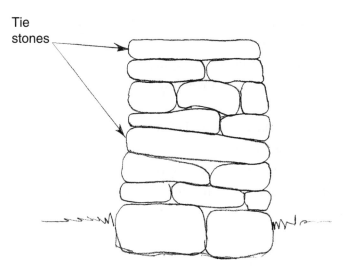

Tie stones

Follow the old masons' rule, "one stone over two, and two stones over one."

Stone can be dry laid to create low walls or fences. Shown is a cross section of a dry-laid stone wall.

Terrace or retaining walls are constructed in much the same manner as for dry-laid or mortared walls. But because of the problems of water and ground pressure, many municipalities strictly govern this type of wall. You will probably need to get a building permit and show the inspector what type of wall you intend to build. Unless you are experienced, this is best left up to the experts. In both instances, the wall should be sloped backward and allowances made to drain water away from behind the wall.

STONE VENEERING

Stones can also be veneered onto other surfaces such as brick and poured concrete. These must be thin veneer-type stones that are adhered in place with a bed of mortar and metal wall anchors fastened to the wall. The courses are laid in the same manner as for laying a wall.

ARTIFICIAL STONE

Artificial stone, such as that from Cultured Stone Corporation, is a blend of Portland cement and lightweight aggregates and iron oxide pigments cast in molds to resemble natural stone. These

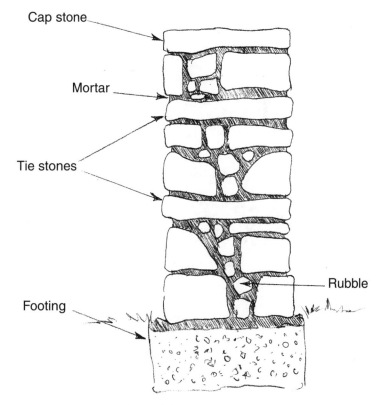

Cap stone

Mortar

Tie stones

Footing

Rubble

Cross-section of a mortared stone wall.

products require no additional footings, foundations, or wall ties and can be installed on a variety of surfaces, including wood framing, rigid foam, and masonry or concrete. A wide variety of shapes, sizes, and colors is available including stones for walls, patios, driveways, walks, and even shaped stone lintels and window moldings. The stones are very consistent in coloring and shapes.

Each piece of Cultured Stone is applied individually with Type N mortar and attached permanently to the wall. Then a mortar joint is grouted between the stones. Some products are also designed to be installed without grouting to create a dry-laid look. Cultured Stone veneers are durable, maintenance free, non-combustible, and are covered by a 30-year limited warranty.

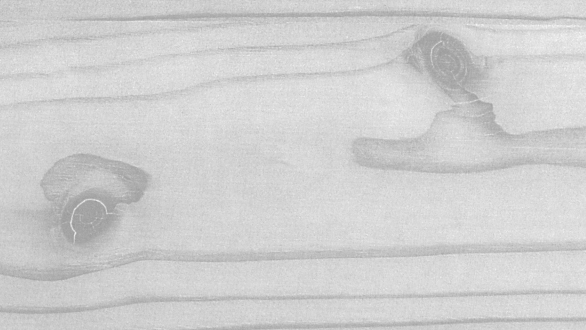

SECTION III

DECKS AND PATIOS

Decks and patios are two of the most popular backyard structures. They can be small extensions off family rooms, bedrooms, or dining areas or they can be spacious outdoor rooms large enough for parties. Decks and patios can be single level or multilevel and they can be some of the simplest "first" projects for a beginner or elaborate examples of sophisticated craftsmanship. For greater versatility, both decks and patios can utilize covers, and decks can create a wealth of under-deck storage.

CHAPTER 1

DECK-BUILDING BASICS

DECKS ARE QUITE OFTEN the first project many beginning do-it-your-selfers tackle. It is important to understand the basics of deck construction. Decks are built in specific steps. By taking those steps one-at-a-time, building a deck can be fun and easy.

PLANNING

The first step is to design and plan your deck. Location is important. Determine the primary use, such as a place for large parties, family relaxing, outdoor cooking, or private sunbathing areas. Do you desire sunlight or shade? Do you want privacy? Is there a view you wish to enjoy? How would the deck fit with your general landscaping? How would the deck fit with your existing structures? Consider the safety factors. Will children or older persons use the deck? Remember decks are basically support bases for people to walk on, as well as to support items such as flower planters and furniture. They must be constructed strong enough for this support. Measure the area of the proposed deck and temporarily stake it out with small stakes. Make sure there are no utility or drainage lines running beneath the deck. Contact the local building authorities for any permits and any code rules or limitations. Some cities, municipalities, communities, or subdivisions may restrict the size and height of the deck, as well as the materials. Determine the basic design of the deck, such as posts, beams, and other spacing, and prepare a materials list. With this basic information you can apply for any permits needed.

Decks are some of the most popular homeowner backyard projects. They can range from the very simple to multi-level, extremely sophisticated projects. (Photo courtesy California Redwood Assoc.)

Decks must be constructed of a long-lasting material. Pressure-treated wood, such as Wolmanized Natural Select, is a good, long-lasting, economical, and readily available decking material. (Photo courtesy Wolmanized Natural Select wood)

Today, composite decking materials are also very popular. They're beautiful, require almost no maintenance, and come in a variety of styles. (Photo courtesy ChoiceDek)

MATERIALS

Decks must be constructed of long-lasting, moisture-resistant, rot-resistant, decay-resistant, and insect-resistant materials. Three basic types of materials can be used: naturally insect- and moisture-resistant woods such as redwood; pressure-treated woods, such as Wolmanized Natural Select; or composite decking materials. Availability, cost, the final design of the deck, as well as personal preferences will determine the materials chosen. Check with your local building supply dealers as to the materials available in your area.

Take the time to design your deck to suit your house location, deck uses, and backyard topography, as well as location in regards to sun and shade.

DESIGN

Regardless of how low or how high, a deck consists of several basic parts: the footings; posts or vertical support members; the beams or horizontal supports; the joists; and the decking and finishing details such as railings and steps. The size and spacing of the different members depend on the design of the deck and the woods being used. The following charts show the spacing for Womanized Natural Select Pressure Treated lumber and non-stress-graded redwood (Construction Heart) lumber.

Suggested Beam Spans

For non-stress-graded redwood lumber (Construction Heart), with a live load of 40 lbs. per sq. ft. and deal load of 10 lbs. per sq. ft.

Beam Spacing		Beam Sizes	
	4 × 6	4 × 8	4 × 10
	Span	Span	Span
6 feet	4' 0"	5' 0"	7' 3"
8 feet	3' 3"	4' 3"	7' 3"
10 feet	3' 0"	3' 9"	5' 6"
12 feet	2' 9"	3' 6"	5' 0"

Beam span is the distance a beam extends from one post to the next. Beam spacing is the distance between beams. Deflection is limited to L/240.

Suggested Joist Spans

For non-stress-graded redwood lumber (Construction Heart) with live load of 40 lbs. per sq. ft.

Joist Size	Joist Spacing	Joist Span
2 × 6	16″ on center	7′ 3″
	24″ on center	6′ 0″
2 × 8	16″ on center	10′ 9″
	24″ on center	8′ 9″
2 × 10	16″ on center	13′ 6″
	24″ on center	11′ 0″

Deflection limited to L/240.

Determining Joist Size

Based on 12″ joist spacing

Max. Joist Span: Southern Pine Hem–Fir	Max. Joist Span: Red Pine Ponderosa Pine	Use Joist Size:
9′	7′ 6″	2 × 6
12′	10′	2 × 8
15′	13′	2 × 10

Based on 16″ joist spacing

Max. Joist Span: Southern Pine Hem–Fir	Max. Joist Span: Red Pine Ponderosa Pine	Use Joist Size:
8′	6′ 6″	2 × 6
10′ 6″	9′	2 × 8
13′	11′ 6″	2 × 10

Based on 24″ joist spacing

Max. Joist Span: Southern Pine Hem–Fir	Max. Joist Span: Red Pine Ponderosa Pine	Use Joist Size:
6′ 6″	NA	2 × 6
8′ 6″	7′	2 × 8
11′	9′	2 × 10

Determining Post Size

Species: Southern Pine and Hem-Fir

Post Height	48	72	96	120	144
			Load Area: sq. ft.		
Up to 6'	4 × 4	4 × 4	4 × 4	4 × 6	4 × 6
Up to 8'	4 × 4	4 × 6	4 × 6	6 × 6	6 × 6

Species: Red Pine and Ponderosa Pine

Post Height	48	72	96	120	144
			Load Area: sq. ft.		
Up to 6'	4 × 4	4 × 4	4 × 4	4 × 6	4 × 6
Up to 8'	4 × 4	4 × 6	4 × 6	6 × 6	6 × 6

Knee bracing should be used for heights over six feet. For heights over eight feet, consult a professional engineer.

These tables are based on a live load of 40 pounds per square foot. If your deck will experience heavier loads, consult an engineer or your lumber dealer for design assistance.

Determining Beam size/Post Spacing

Species: Southern Pine and Hem-Fir

If joist size is:	Use beam size of:	Max. post spacing
2 × 6	(2) 2 × 6	6'
	(2) 2 × 8	8'
2 × 8	(2) 2 × 8	6'
	(2) 2 × 10	8'
2 × 10	(2) 2 × 10	6'
	(2) 2 × 12	8'

Species: Red Pine and Ponderosa Pine

If joist size is:	Use beam size of:	Max. post spacing
2 × 6	(2) 2 × 6	5'
	(2) 2 × 8	7'
2 × 8	(2) 2 × 8	5'
	(2) 2 × 10	7'
2 × 10	(2) 2 × 10	5'
	(2) 2 × 12	7'

LAYING OUT THE DECK

It is important to lay out the deck square, and it also must be square with any building it is to be attached to. Even if part of the deck is free form or rounded, the basic support structure must be squared.

The first step is to determine the height of the deck. If the deck is to be attached to a house or building, measure the height of the house floor above your grade line or at the doorway. Allow a 2- to 4-inch step down from the house floor to the deck level so water won't be allowed to enter the building. Next, measure one side to the length needed and drive a stake. Fasten a string to the house at the height determined. Using a string level to create a level line and fasten the string to the stake. Measure for the second corner stake, making sure the measurements are the same. Then measure the distance between the two lines attached to the house and adjust the outrigger stakes so they are the same distance apart. This provides the basic shape. Drive stakes and construct batter boards about 2 feet on either side of the outer stakes. Before fastening the batter boards in place to the stakes, extend string lines across to the batter board tops and, using a string level, make sure the tops of the batter boards are level with the string positions on the house and level with each other.

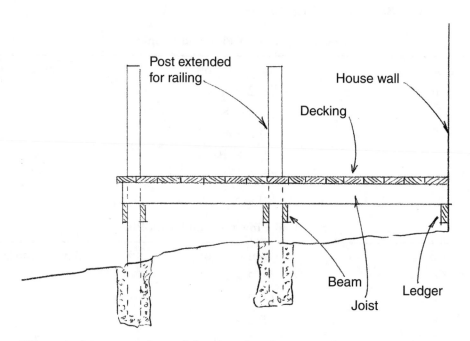

Whatever its design, size, or shape, a deck consists of specific parts, including the support posts, ledger board, beams, joists, covering, and often railings and steps.

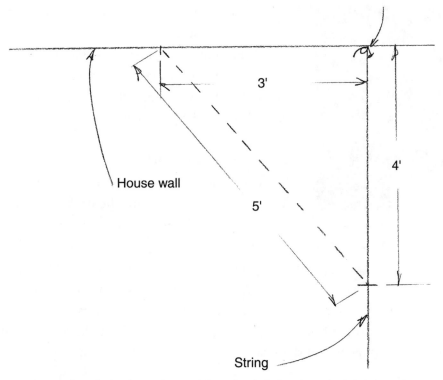

3'

4'

5'

House wall

String

Use the triangle method and string lines with batter boards for laying out the deck, locating the posts and assuring the deck support structure is created "square."

One method of ensuring square is to create a right angle with the string lines. Measure 3 feet from the building, along the string, and mark this distance with a felt tip pen. Measure 4 feet along the building wall and mark that measurement as well. Measure diagonally between the two marks. The measurement must be 5 feet to create a square corner. Move the string line in or out to achieve the correct measurement. Then fasten the string in the correct location to the batter board. This creates a square corner at the building. Repeat for the opposite edge or side of the deck, from the building out to the second outer stake batter board.

Repeat to locate the outer deck edge. Measure 4 feet from where the string lines cross over the tops of the outside corner stakes along one of the string lines. Mark this location with a felt-tip marker. Measure 3 feet from where the string lines cross on the opposite line and mark this location as well. Measure the distance diagonally between the two marks. It must be 5 feet. Move the strings in or out until you achieve this measurement. This ensures a square 90-degree corner at this corner. Repeat for the opposite and last corner. Remove the stakes and relocate them directly under where each string crosses. This establishes the outside corners. To check for squareness, measure diagonally

The new Craftsman LaserTrac 360-degree Rotary Laser System makes it easy to level the support system for decks. It features three rotary or spinning speeds to adjust the laser line for optimum visibility.

between each corner stake and the deck corner at the house. These measurements should be equal.

To prevent weeds from growing up through the deck, you may wish to cover the area below the deck with black polyethylene film then add gravel, pebbles or bark mulch over the polyethylene.

DECK CONSTRUCTION

The first construction step consists of installing a ledger board, the support for the deck as it is fastened to the building. Position the ledger board in place against the house, making sure it is set low enough for the top decking boards to come to the final deck height. Brace the ledger board in place, make sure it is level, and then nail it in place at both ends, again making sure it is still level. Anchor the ledger firmly to the house using washers and ⅜-inch lag bolts that are 2 inches longer than the thickness of the ledger. For masonry walls, use the appropriate masonry anchors.

Footings are required to support the posts. These may be concrete blocks, precast pier blocks, or poured concrete supports. Footings are usually constructed twice the size of the post it supports. Building codes usually dictate the types and sizes of footings allowed. As a rule, the footings must extend below the frost line. In most soils and locations this will be 2 feet deep. The tops of the footings should be above the ground to keep water away from the posts. In the case of using pressure-treated wood posts, the posts can be set down in the holes, on a layer of concrete, then a layer of gravel. QUIKRETE suggests pouring dry concrete mix into the hole and around the post until it is approximately 3 to 4 inches from the top. Two 50-pound bags of QUIKRETE Fast-Setting Concrete Mix will set a 4 × 4 (or 4-inch diameter) post in a 10-inch diameter hole that's 2 feet deep. Pour water into the dry mix and allow it to soak in. Use at least 1 gallon of water per each 50-pound bag of concrete. Fill the remainder of the hole with soil dug from the hole. The concrete sets up in about 20 to 40 minutes. Wait 4 hours before placing heavy objects on the post or moving the posts in any way.

Purchased pier footings are the easiest, but pouring your own concrete footings for posts to rest on is also fairly easy. These can be poured in the dug holes or cardboard "Sona" tube forms may be used. Use pre-mixed concrete, such as QUICKRETE, mixing it in a wheelbarrow and shoveling it into the hole or tube form. If the posts do not sit down in the holes, but are resting on the aboveground footing tops, then the posts must

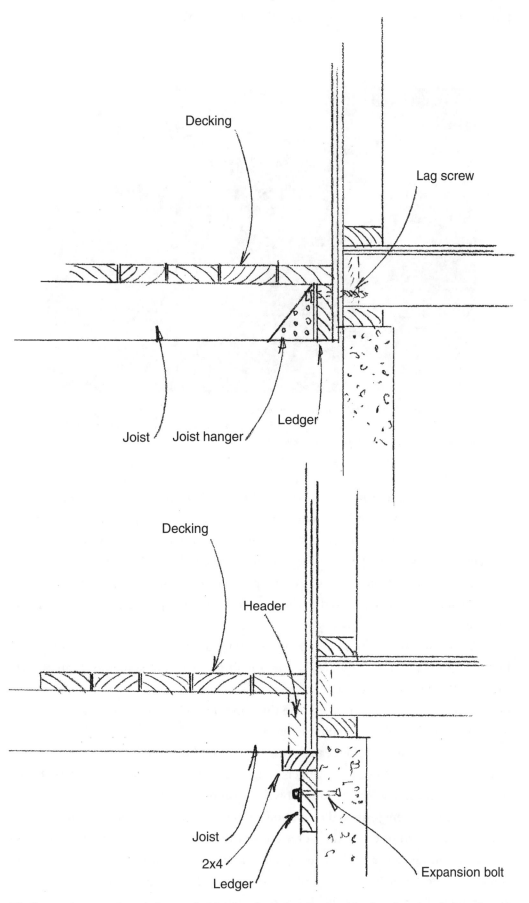

Decking

Lag screw

Joist   Joist hanger   Ledger

Decking

Header

Joist

2x4

Ledger

Expansion bolt

The first step in constructing a deck onto a building is to fasten the ledger board in place. Several methods can be used, depending on the type of house construction.

The Craftsman 14.4-Volt EX Impact Driver makes short work of driving lag screws to fasten ledger boards or beams in place. The variable-speed ¼-inch reversible driver revolves and impacts simultaneously and delivers up to 850 pounds of torque.

be anchored to the footing. Metal base anchors, such as those from Simpson Strong-Tie Connectors, can be set in the concrete before it sets up. The posts are then fastened to the anchors. Whether the posts are setting in the holes or on the footings, it's extremely important to make sure the posts are correctly located, and the squareness of the structure is maintained. Make sure the posts are set plumb in both directions. Use 2-×-4 braces temporarily tacked to the posts to keep them plumb until you can install the beams or girders.

To locate the beams, run a string line, with a string level, from the top of the house ledger plate to the posts. Make sure the line is level. Three methods can be used to fasten the beams in place. If there won't be a railing, cut off the posts to attach the beams, cutting off to match one of the three methods chosen. If a railing is involved, leave the posts full height as railing supports.

Fasten the joists to the beams. One of two methods can be used to anchor the joists in place. Using metal joist hangers is the simplest, cutting the joists to fit between the beams. You can also sit the joists down on top of the ledger plate and outer beam, but this requires more joists and is not quite as neat in appearance. You will also have to have a fascia board to cover the outer ends of the exposed joists. The joists must be spaced according to the deck covering and according to building codes and this will run from 16 to 24 inches. If the posts are to act as railing supports, add spacer railing-posts, bolting them to the outside beam or girder.

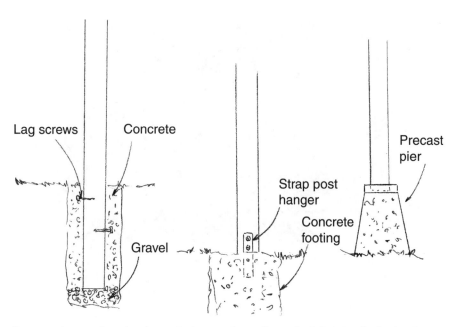

Posts must be properly anchored or set in the ground, according to the deck design, local code rules, type of soil, and geographic location.

INSTALLING THE DECKING

Decking can be 2-✕-4, 2-✕-6, or 5/4 decking boards. The decking is the most visible aspect of your deck. Install it with care. Begin with the deck board perpendicular to the house. This board will serve as the guide board for all the other deck boards. Install the boards "bark-side" up to reduce cupping of the board edges. Install the decking with

Once the support system is constructed, the decking boards are installed. The Magnesium Coil Utility Nailer from Craftsman is lightweight, easy-to-use, and drives smooth, ring, or spiral shank nails.

A wide variety of screws, especially those designed for use with the newer versions of treated wood, such as the Stanley-Bostitch fasteners with THICKCOAT *galvanization, can also be used for fastening decks together. (Photo Courtesy Stanley-Bostitch)*

galvanized nails, screws, or Strong-Tie Deck Board Ties. The latter provides a fastener-free deck surface. Although the most economical, nails will eventually pop up, causing problems. Predrill nails on certain woods to prevent splitting out the ends. For more variety, you can install deck boards straight, diagonal, herringbone, or parquet-style. Whichever style you use, stagger the deck boards to allow for any slight movement during the natural seasoning process. Once installed, you can snap a chalk line on the sides or ends where the boards protrude outside the deck and then, with a circular saw, cut all the boards off evenly. You will have to notch decking boards to fit around any posts that protrude through the deck. Incidentally, the Vaughn Bowjak makes it easy to straighten and hold warped or crooked deck boards until they can be securely fastened in place.

DECK-FINISHING DETAILS

Steps are often needed from the deck to ground level or from one deck level to the next. Steps can be created using a traditional notched stringer system, or you can use Strong-Tie Connector Stair Case Angles. These make it extremely easy to adjust the angle of the stringers to span the distance from the deck to the ground. Measure the rise (vertical height) from grade top to the top of the deck. Divide the rise by 7 inches or whatever stair rise you prefer. This indicates how many stair risers are required. To determine the total run of the stairs, multiply the number of steps required by 11¼ inches. Cut the 2-×-10 stair stringers and fasten to the deck framing with a Strong-Tie

A cordless jigsaw is extremely handy for notching deck boards around posts and other chores.

Framing Anchor. Mark the staircase angle support position on both stringers. Install the Staircase Angles with ¼-×-1½ inch lag screws and then fasten the stair treads in place. If more than three steps are involved, a hand railing should be added to each side.

Railings not only provide safety to higher decks, but also add to the "décor." Most building codes call for a railing if the deck is more than 24 inches off the ground. In the past, railings tended to be straight wood pieces. These days, a wide range of railing designs is available, including turned spindles and supports from BW Creative Wood.

The Craftsman LaserTrac circular saw with a laser-guided line makes it easy to trim the ends of deck boards.

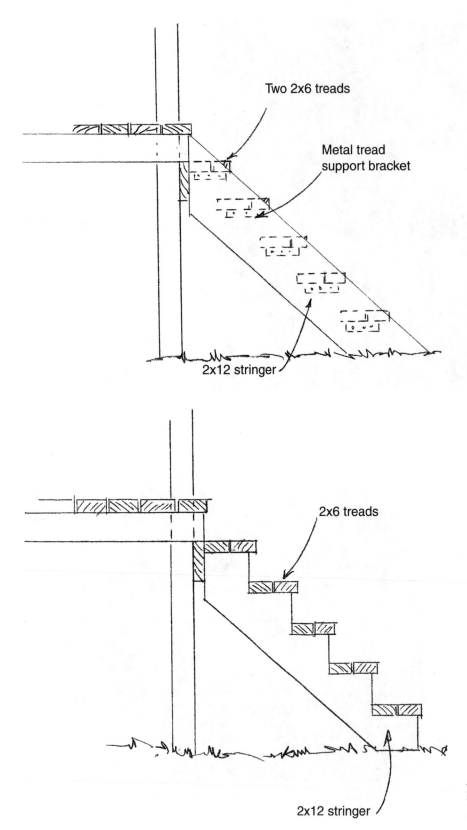

Two 2x6 treads

Metal tread
support bracket

2x12 stringer

2x6 treads

2x12 stringer

A wide variety of finishing details can add to the deck, including steps, railings, planters, and seats. (Figure continued on next page.)

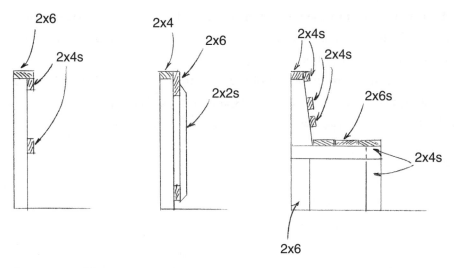

(Figure continued from previous page.)

COMPOSITE DECKING

Composite deck materials, including deck flooring, rails, and balusters, require some-what different steps in installation. The different products from the many different man-ufacturers do require specific installation and construction steps. Most posts and rails come as a "system." Make sure you carefully follow the manufacturer's instructions with the products purchased. This includes design, such as spacing of the railings, and so forth. Composite materials are not designed for load support. Whatever composite decking and railing system you choose, it must first be supported on a wooden frame-work, in the same construction manner as for a full-wood deck. Following are a few tips on installation of the ChoiceDek system from Weyerhaeuser.

The first step is to assemble the post bracket and fasten to the rim joists. Insert posts into the brackets and connect with the appropriate fasteners. Then install the decking materials, cutting to fit around the posts and leaving a ⅛-inch gap. For a more decorative look, add a post collar over the post. Then attach edge trim to the ends of the decking boards.

Measure and cut the universal support rails and the decorative handrail. Attach with the brackets supplied. Support blocks to match the balusters are suggested for extra strength. Insert the end balusters/spindles tight against the posts, then insert the balusters and fillets to space them properly. Fasten in place with stainless steel fasteners. Fillet spacer blocks may also be glued in place. Install the decorative handrail. Then cut the post tops to the correct size if you haven't already done so. Install the post caps.

Stair railings are installed in the same manner, except with one difference, they're on an angle. Installation requires additional care in measuring, cutting, and fitting. The posts are first anchored to the stair stringers. Then the decking material for the steps is installed. Again, the universal stair rails are then installed, followed by the balusters, fillets, decorative handrail, and post tops.

Don't be limited in the design of the deck to a floor only. Planter boxes, built-in bench seating, privacy screens, deck covers, and even pool and spa surrounds can all add to the beauty, usefulness, and enjoyment of a deck for your backyard.

CHAPTER 2

DECK AND PATIO SUNSHADES

YOU CAN ADD TO the enjoyment of patios and decks by providing shade over them, or over portions of the areas. Patios and decks are often constructed to take advantage of natural shade from trees or even an adjacent building; however, constructing a sunshade structure is an alternative. Sunshades can be quite simple or extremely elaborate. They can provide partial shade only with the use of latticework, or they can also support a roof to provide both sun and weather protection. And they can be constructed free standing or they can be attached to a building.

You can make your patio or deck more enjoyable with a redwood sunshade. (Photo courtesy California Redwood Assoc.)

CONSTRUCTING LOUVER/LATTICE SUNSHADES

Lattice sunshades utilize parallel-placed louver boards or constructed lattice to break up the sun's rays. These shades are extremely easy to construct and may be free standing or attached to a building. You can use a variety of board sizes and patterns or you can

California redwood is an excellent choice for sunshades. It's naturally insect-and decay-resistant, and it has a beautiful color. (Photo courtesy California Redwood Assoc.)

With redwood, a wide variety of designs and construction features can be used. (Photo courtesy California Redwood Assoc.)

Sunshades can be freestanding, with minimum shade provision. (Photo courtesy Wolmanized Natural Select wood)

purchase manufactured redwood lattice. The manufactured lattice may not be feasible in areas with heavy snow loads, however.

In most instances some or all of the sunshade will be supported by posts. These posts must be set in or on concrete footings to properly support the structure. Check with local building codes for footing requirements in your area. Posts may be embedded in concrete, anchored to concrete piers with metal anchors, or in some instances, even bolted to the deck floor joists. This latter method depends on the deck construction and local building codes. When installing the posts, use a 4-foot level to make sure they are plumb and then temporarily brace the posts in place. Trim the posts to final height if necessary. These types of structures do not need water run-off so they are made flat with no "roof pitch."

In many instances the sunshade will be connected to a building. In this case, a ledger, or support board, must be attached to the house or building. The structure joist ends are supported by the ledger board. The ledger must be attached to the house wall

Sunshades can also be attached to an existing building. (Photo courtesy California Redwood Assoc.)

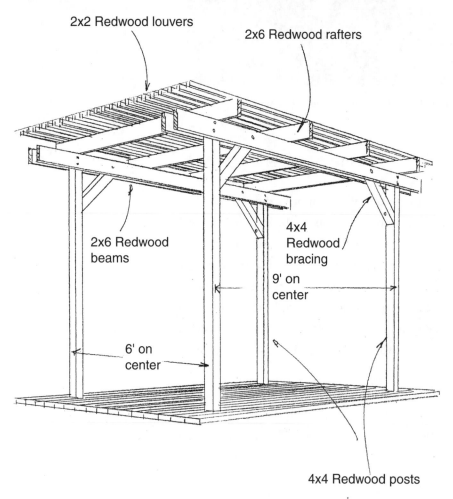

2x2 Redwood louvers

2x6 Redwood rafters

2x6 Redwood beams

4x4 Redwood bracing

9' on center

6' on center

4x4 Redwood posts

A small shade, such as this redwood freestanding unit, is fairly easy to construct.

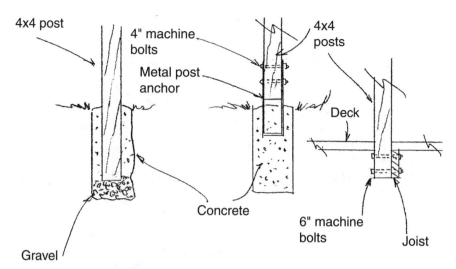

The structure is supported on 4-x-4 redwood posts. The posts must be securely anchored. Check with local building codes for rules and regulations.

studs, and/or door or window headers with 4-inch lag bolts. If connecting to a header, space bolts no more than 24 inches on center. Acrylic latex or polyurethane caulk should be used to seal the top joint where the ledger meets the sidewall of the house as well as to seal the lag bolts and holes.

The next step is to install the support beams. These are 2 × 6s attached to each set of posts, or to the front posts if an attached sunshade is being constructed. Position and

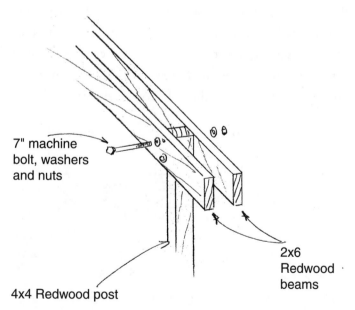

Redwood beams are then fastened to the posts with machine bolts.

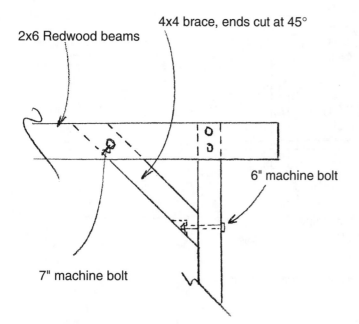

2x6 Redwood beams

4x4 brace, ends cut at 45°

6" machine bolt

7" machine bolt

Four-by-four redwood braces are bolted to the beams and posts.

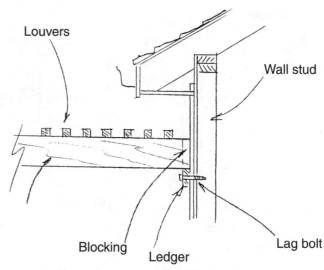

Louvers

Wall stud

Blocking

Ledger

Lag bolt

If the structure is to be fastened to a building, a ledger board is first anchored to the building to support the rafters.

then fasten the beams to the posts with brass deck screws, making sure the beams are even with the tops of the posts. Then drill two ½-inch diameter holes through both the beams and each post. Use 7-inch machine bolts to secure the beams solidly in place.

The corners of a freestanding or the front corners of an attached sunshade must be braced with 45-degree angle braces cut from 4 × 4s. Attach the braces with one end between the support beams, using a 7-inch machine bolt. Fasten the opposite end to the upright post with a 6-inch machine bolt countersunk in place. Next, install 2-×-6 rafters, 18 inches apart, over the beams. The rafters may be toenailed with nails or fastened with deck screws. Use one fastener on each side of the board into both support beams on either side. Pre-drill the holes to prevent splitting out the boards. Metal

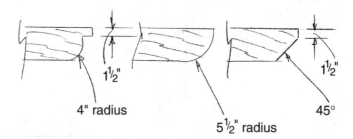

1½"

4" radius

5½" radius

1½"

45°

The rafter ends may be cut in a variety of ways to add to or match your décor.

rafter supports can also be used, but they may detract from the appearance. Once the rafters are in place you can remove the post bracing pieces.

The last construction step is to attach the top. This top may be louvers, ready-made lattice, or you can custom-make your own lattice. Louvers are constructed by ripping materials into 2 × 2s that are actually 1½ × 1½ inches. Attach the louvers to the rafters, leaving an overhang of 18 inches. Locate the position of the rafters on the louvers, lay the louvers side by side, and pre-drill the fastener holes. Then attach the louvers with 8d nails or brass deck screws. The spacing of the louvers determines the amount of shade the shelter will provide. Spacing the louvers 3 inches on center provides quite a bit of shade. Four-inch spacing provides more of a filtered light.

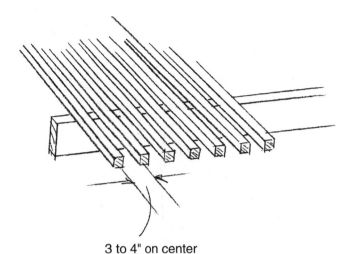

3 to 4" on center

One of the most common methods of providing shade is with 2-x-2 redwood "louvers" anchored to the rafters.

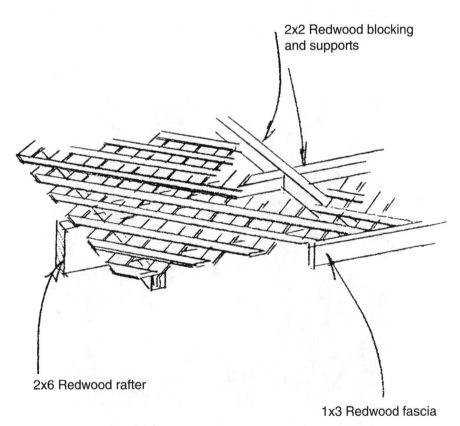

2x2 Redwood blocking and supports

2x6 Redwood rafter

1x3 Redwood fascia

Purchased redwood lattice can be used in areas without snow loads.

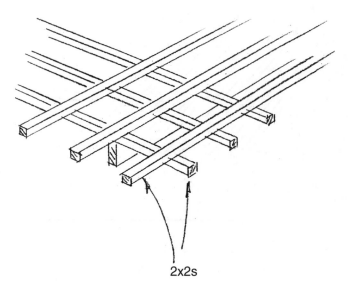

You can custom-build your own lattice from 2 x 2s.

Readymade redwood lattice can also be applied. This provides a moderate amount of shading, with an interesting shade pattern thrown on the deck or patio. To support and join the edges of the lattice sheets, install 2-×-2 redwood blocking between the rafters. The lattice should be anchored with non-corrosive nails or screws. You can also create your own custom lattice design using 2 × 2s.

CONSTRUCTING A COVERED SUNSHADE

A covered sunshade not only provides sun protection, but weather protection as well. There are many methods you can use to construct one. A solid roof can be installed, or you can utilize a variety of shade materials such as PVC corrugated panels. Suntuf Sun 'N Rain PVC panels are tough, lightweight, and highly durable. They are weather- and corrosion-proof, UV-inhibited, and provide for natural soft light transmission. The residential D.I.Y. panels are available in many profiles, including graceful round waves. The panels come in either translucent or opaque and

Sunshades can also provide water and weather protection if the framing is covered with materials such as Suntuf Sun 'N Rain PVC panels. (Photo Courtesy Suntuf, Inc.)

Covering a play area with Suntuf polycarbonate panels can provide necessary protection. They won't allow harmful UV radiation through. (Photo Courtesy Suntuf, Inc.)

an assortment of colors. They measure 26 inches in width and are sold in standard lengths of 8, 10, and 12 feet.

Construction of the supporting members is basically the same as for the uncovered sunshade, but you must take into account snow loads in areas with snowfall. Make sure you check with local building codes on footings, support posts, and rafter spacing. Sun'N Rain suggests rafters run 16 to 24 inches with a minimum of 24-inch distance between purlin headers for snow load areas. The roof will also require a "pitch" to ensure water runoff. This is the amount of height in inches the rafter rises over a 12-inch run. Minimum pitch suggested is 1½ inches in 12 inches. Project accessories include nails and wood or foam closure strips as well as 1¾-inch neoprene roofing nails designed specially for use with Sun 'N Rain panels. The opaque panels are suitable for all weather conditions, but the clear panels must be installed in mild weather conditions only. The clear panels should not be installed in locations with high UV radiation or temperatures above 130 degrees F.

Closure strips, either wood or foam, are used horizontally under the panels as fastener supports. Foam closures are recommended because they can be stretched tightly to align with the panels to form a compression fit. Suntuf Neoprene Washered fasteners must be used. Pre-drill all fastener holes with a ³⁄₁₆-inch drill bit to accommodate for thermal movement of the panels. Long-length panels should have holes over-drilled. Failure to do so will not accommodate thermal movement and cause buckling of the panels. Attach fasteners on the crown of every other rib in the horizontal direction. High-wind areas should have the fasteners on the crown of every rib. Do not over-tighten the fasteners, which can cause the rubber washer to compress. Back out the fastener a half turn after the neoprene washer touches the panel (the neoprene washer should just touch the panel). Panels can be cut with a circular saw with a plywood blade reversed, a utility knife and a straight edge, or a pair of snips. Support the sheets to avoid vibration and cut at a slow speed.

With a little effort, you can enjoy both the shade and sun on your patio or deck this summer.

CHAPTER 3

UNDER-DECK STORAGE

IN THE PAST, MANY aboveground pool owners eventually built a deck around all or a portion of their pools. Today many aboveground pools come complete with a freestanding deck surround. Most pool surrounds or decks for 4-foot deep pools, the most common, are between 3 and 4 feet high. The surround shown is somewhat typical and, although custom built, the space under the deck is wasted. Building a storage area beneath provides storage for pool, deck, and garden supplies and equipment. Although the storage unit shown is built to suit the specific deck, the same construction can be used to create a storage unit for any deck—merely change the dimensions to suit. For instance, the unit can be made wider, deeper, shallower, or taller, depending on the situation. The top is sloped to allow rainwater to run off. The unit is designed to fit just under the deck joist. A 2-×-4-support strip is fastened to the front of the deck posts to support the front of the unit. The bottom is supported under the deck on concrete blocks. Additional support can be provided by strap hangers anchored to the deck underside and to the storage unit sides or end. The unit is positioned in place with its front edge flush with the deck posts and support boards. You may need to build out the posts with a 2 × 4 to make sure they're flush with the upper and lower support boards.

The entire storage unit is constructed of pressure-treated materials for longevity. Pressure-treated plywood is used for the sides, end, bottom, top, and door, as well as the door trim. Galvanized deck screws are used for the entire construction. The inside is framed with 2 × 4s and 2 × 2s.

First, cut the sides to shape. With the plywood positioned on a pair of sawhorses, mark the shape using a straight edge or chalk line. With the work piece well supported,

Under-deck pool and deck storage provides handy space for pool chemicals and deck objects. Made of pressure-treated wood, the unit is fastened to the deck and supported in the rear on 4-inch solid concrete blocks.

Some portions of the interior framing utilize 2 x 2s ripped from 2 x 4s. A portable circular saw and rip guide makes the chore easy.

make the cut. Note, as you continue the cut, the cut plywood edges will sag and can cause the saw to kick back dangerously out of the work. Prevent this by placing a brace beneath the beginning of the cut and across the sawhorses to support the cut edges.

With the rip gauge on a portable circular saw, or using a table or radial arm saw, rip 4s into the 2s needed for the inside supports. Measure and cut the front side supports to length, angling the top ends slightly to allow for the sloping roof, about 10 degrees. It's a good idea to cut both front side supports, and then cut the back side supports while the saw is set at the angle needed. Fasten the front edge of the sides to the side supports with their 4 inches facing outward. Fasten the 2-×-2 back side supports to the sides. Measure and cut a 2-×-2 top and 2-×-4 bottom side support for each side and fasten to the side and uprights.

Cut the 2-X-4 front bottom and top support. Place the side assemblies on a smooth, flat surface, such as a garage floor, and, with someone helping hold them upright, fasten the front support pieces between the sides with ¼-X-6 inch lag bolts and washers. Cut the back top and bottom support pieces to length and fasten with ¼-X-4 inch lag bolts and washers. Cut a center floor joist and fasten between the front and rear bottom supports.

A portable circular saw is used to cut the ½-inch plywood needed to cover the assembly.

Cut the bottom to size, making sure it is cut square, and then cut notches around the front and rear upright support pieces. Fasten the bottom in place.

Cut a 2-X-4 center rafter and anchor between the top and rear upper supports. The center rafter will have a slight angle to fit properly and follow the roof slope. Cut the roof to size. Apply a bead of caulking around the top supports to provide further rain protection, and then install the roof.

Galvanized deck screws, cordless electric drill, and Craftsman Speed-Lok System makes assembly quick and easy.

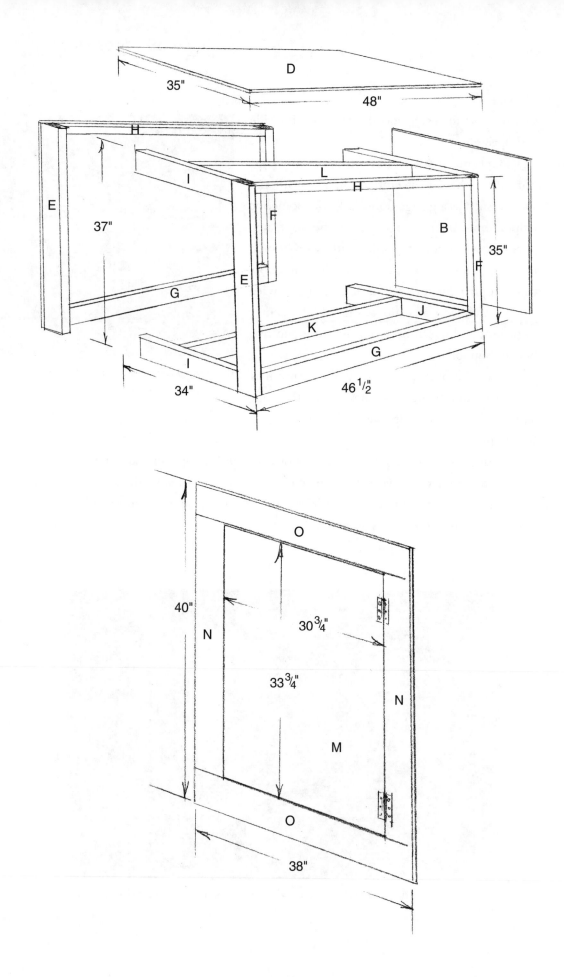

D

35"

48"

H

I

L

H

E

37"

F

B

35"

E

G

F

J

K

G

I

34"

46 1/2"

O

40"

N

30 3/4"

33 3/4"

N

M

O

38"

Now comes the hard part. The assembly is fairly heavy and help will be needed to get the assembly moved and positioned under the deck. Position the four concrete block supports under the deck, one in each corner. Place the back edge of the assembly on the deck lower support board, and then slide the unit in place onto the concrete blocks. The front edge of the unit must be flush with the outside edge of the deck pieces. Dig down or add pressure-treated shims to level the blocks if necessary. A sturdy pry bar may be needed to lift the rear of the storage unit for leveling. Make sure the storage unit is installed plumb.

The door can be hinged to swing in either direction. Cut the hinge-side trim piece. Anchor the trim piece to the storage unit and the deck support post, overlapping the deck post by 1½ inches. Cut the door, which is ¼ inch smaller than the door opening, and hinge to the hinge-side trim. The screws will protrude slightly through the back side and the sharp points should be ground down with a hand grinder such as a Dremel.

Fasten the latch-side trim piece to the unit front and the deck post. Install the latch and grind the screw points inside the door. Cut and install the upper and lower trim pieces, again fastening to the storage unit and to the deck supports.

Customize the interior of the storage unit to suit your particular storage needs. Stain or paint the unit and trim to match the deck or to match your house trim.

Materials List

(Note the dimensions and drawing are for a unit with outside measurements of 35 inches wide, 37½ inches tall, and 47½ inches deep.)

A. sides: ½ in. plywood, 37 × 46½ in., 2 req'd
B. back: ½ in. plywood, 35 × 35 in., 1 req'd
C. bottom: ½ in. plywood, 34 × 46½ in., cut to fit, 1 req'd
D. top: ½ in. plywood, 35 × 48 in., 1 req'd
E. front side supports: 2 × 4 × 37 in., 2 req'd
F. rear side supports: 2 × 2 × 35 in., 2 req'd
G. bottom side supports: 2 × 4 × 43½ in., 2 req'd
H. top side supports: 2 × 2 × 44 in., cut to fit, 2 req'd
I. bottom and top front supports: 2 × 4 × 27 in., 1 each req'd
J. bottom and top rear supports: 2 × 4 × 31 in., 1 each req'd
K. floor joist: 2 × 4 × 43½ in., 1 req'd
L. rafter: 2 × 4 × 44 in., cut to fit, 1 req'd
M. door: ½ in. plywood, 30¾ × 33¾ in., 1 req'd
N. side trim pieces: ½ in. plywood, 3 × 34 in., 2 req'd
O. upper and lower trim pieces: ½ in. plywood, 3 × 38 in., 2 req'd

BACKYARD DÉCOR

Building small backyard projects to provide décor or for practical use is a rewarding woodworking hobby. Picnic tables, garden benches, trellises, and planters have all been popular projects for many years. Shown are some fairly traditional designs, along with a few unusual ones.

CHAPTER 1

BACKYARD PLANTERS

WHEN I WAS A KID, one of my jobs was to mow my aunt's yard. My aunt loved flowers. She stuck a flower here, one there, another over there. I was perpetually in trouble for mowing over what I *thought* were weeds. These days, my wife loves flowers as much as my aunt did but, for the most part, she has our flowers organized into beds and planters. I still can't guarantee her that I will never again mow down a promising specimen, but I'm no longer the menace I was to my aunt's blossoms. Planters or organized beds with planter borders can provide not only mowing definition, but also contain the flowers and help keep out weeds that may grow into them from surrounding areas. And backyard planters can be big or small, permanent or portable.

The simplest planters consist of edging for flower or vegetable beds. In the past, many gardeners used recycled railroad ties for this, and they still add a distinctive rustic appeal to garden beds. In recent years, however, pressure-treated landscaping timbers have become increasingly popular. These are also very easy to use to create bed edges, or even to build up permanent planters. Railroad ties usually have enough weight to stay in place when used in a single layer as an edging material. Landscaping timbers are usually smaller and they can be shifted by the weight of the soil in the planter, although even railroad timbers can shift over time. One solution is to bore holes down through the timbers or ties and drive 12-inch long sections of ⅜-inch concrete reinforcing rod down through the wood and into the ground. Make sure you set the ends of the rods below the wood surface so that no rough metal edges protrude.

The simplest planters are bed edgings. These can be recycled railroad ties or the more modern landscaping ties.

Regardless of which is used, one method of keeping the ties in place is to counterbore holes through their tops.

In many instances landscaping timbers or ties are also stacked on top of each other to create deeper planters or beds. The same fastening technique can be used. You may prefer to use 4- to 6-inch ⅜-inch lag screws to bolt landscape timbers together. The corners may be joined with butt joints, overlapped log cabin–style, or mitered and anchored with lag screws. Or, you can use long sections of reinforcing bars cut to fit the height and driven into the ground beneath the planter.

Drive sections of reinforcing bar down through the holes and into the ground.

Joints can be further strengthened by fastening with brass deck screws.

Another common and very attractive permanent bed or edging is stone. Stone can be dry-laid or mortared in place to create all sorts of planter designs.

Portable planters offer the opportunity to place flowers in any location you de-sire. A wide variety of manufactured pots and planters are available for this use. You can even recycle used items into planters. I've seen just about everything you can imagine turned into planters, including an old cast-iron bathtub and even an old commode. The latter didn't look especially attractive to me, but I'm sure the owner had a whimsical

Larger planters can be created by stacking the ties and anchoring them together.

You can also make simple planters from deck floorboards.

mind. Rusty old wheelbarrows, metal watering cans, toy wagons, and other "antiques" can be recycled into planters.

You can also make up your own wooden planters. When assembling wooden planters, use a long-lasting wood that doesn't rot very quickly because it will be constantly exposed to moisture. Western white cedar is one good wood that can be used for these projects. It's quite often used as roof decking, so it's also readily available at most lumber dealers. Pressure-treated wood is also an excellent choice. Excellent planters can also be made from ¾-inch decking boards. They're easy to work with and you can use scraps from finishing a deck to build planters that complement it.

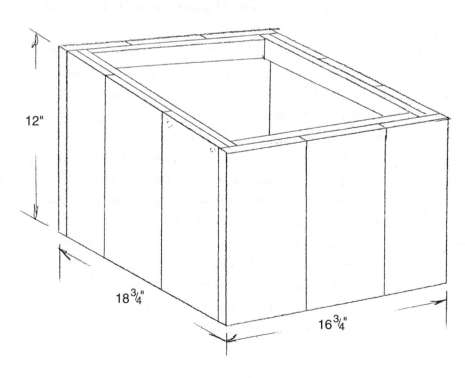

Side cleats are screwed to the side pieces.

The planter shown is very easy to make and, although the design shown is a basic square, you can vary the dimensions to make rectangular short boxes, large and deep patio boxes, and even tall planter boxes with false bottoms to add variety to your backyard deck or patio.

The first step is to cut all of the sidepieces to length. Next, rip the top and bottom side cleats to width. Lay out the pieces for one side on a flat surface. Measure the width and cut a bottom and topside cleat to length. Locate the top cleat flush with the top edge of the sidepieces. Fasten in place with self-starting brass wood deck screws through the cleat into the sidepieces. Locate the bottom-side cleat with its bottom edge flush with the bottom edges of the sidepieces and fasten in place. Repeat for the opposite side. Lay out the sidepieces for a joining side. Cut the bottom-side cleat to length. Note that the cleat is shorter than the thickness of the other two bottom cleats as well as the sidepieces. This allows the first two assembled sides to overlap the next two. Center the cleat in place and fasten it to the sidepieces. Repeat for the opposite side. Fasten the four side assemblies together with brass screws. Cut a pressure-treated bottom from plywood, or use pieces of deck board cut to length and ripped to fit. Bore drain holes in the bottom and then fit the bottom down in place over the bottom cleats. Cut the top cleats to fit between the existing top cleats and fasten to the sidepieces.

Then the sides are assembled. The bottom is positioned before the sides are assembled.

While in Canada recently, I saw a porch railing covered with two types of hanging flower planters. One kind sat on the deck and the other hung from the deck top. A series of boxes, alternating the designs, allowed for a sort of draping arrangement that was very attractive.

Both planters should be made of lightweight materials such as western white cedar. The rail box is constructed so the bottom width is the same as your particular porch or deck rail. The sides extend down over the railing to secure the box in place. You can also add brass deck screws for semi-permanent installation. To remove and clean each year, simply remove the screws. The box is assembled with brass deck screws.

The hanging box is made the same size, except the sides are square with the bottom. Strap iron hangers are bent to hook over the railing and the hangers are then fastened to the back of the planter. Drain holes should be bored in the bottoms of both types of planters. When finished, paint these planters a color to match your house trim for a custom look.

One unusual portable planter I concocted this past summer was created using landscaping timbers. This allowed the planter to be placed in conjunction with the timbers edging a bed. The planter is a hexagon built of small pieces of the timbers. The planter consists of "layers" of octagons stacked up to create the height. For more "flair," the layers are alternated to provide an unusual corner detail. The same octagon design could be stacked with corners mating as well. Regardless of the design, the layers are fastened together from the bottom, starting by placing the top layer upside down. Place

Rail planters can be very attractive on deck and porch rails.

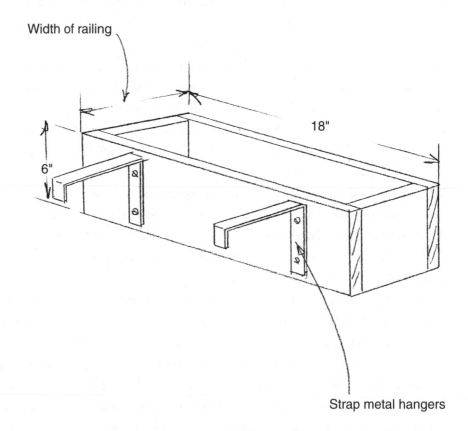

Width of railing

18"

6"

Strap metal hangers

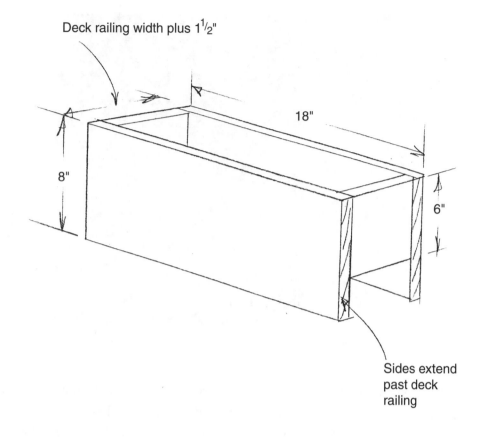

Deck railing width plus 1¹/₂"

18"

8"

6"

Sides extend
past deck
railing

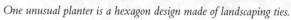

One unusual planter is a hexagon design made of landscaping ties.

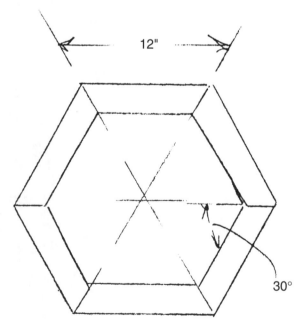

12"

30°

The planter is assembled upside-down. Holes are counterbored for screws.

the next-to-top layer on top of it, lining up the corners as desired. Counter-bore holes through the next-to-top layer into the top layer and fasten with brass screws. A ½-inch pressure-treated plywood bottom was fastened into a rabbet routed around the inside bottom edges of the bottom layer.

With a little imagination, railroad ties, landscaping timbers, piles of stone, or some wood scraps, you can create any number of planters, large and small, for your backyard.

Brass screws are used to assemble the hexagon rings.

CHAPTER 2

GARDEN TRELLISES

SOME OF THE EASIEST and most fun projects to build are garden trellises. Trellises can be used for roses, clematis, and even vegetables such as beans. The materials should, of course, be of pressure-treated wood or other long-lasting material. The trellises can be left in the natural, stained, or painted to suit. Several different and traditional designs are shown.

STRAIGHT TRELLIS

A straight trellis is the simplest. It took me less than an hour to build this model. The first step is to rip the thin strips to the correct width. Cut the verticals to the correct length and lay out on a smooth flat surface. Space the verticals the proper distance apart. Cut the horizontals to the correct length and position them over the verticals. Use a carpenter's square to assure the verticals and all horizontals of the trellis are square, and then fasten in place with self-starting exterior wood screws.

The trellis shown is held upright against a building using 1-×-2-×-12-inch wooden stakes driven into the ground and the trellis screwed to the stakes.

Materials List
verticals: ½ × ¾ × 72 in., 2 req'd
horizontals: ½ × ¾ × 30 in., 5 req'd
support stake: ¾ × 2 × 12 in., 2 req'd

Straight trellis works well with roses, but would be equally good for clematis.

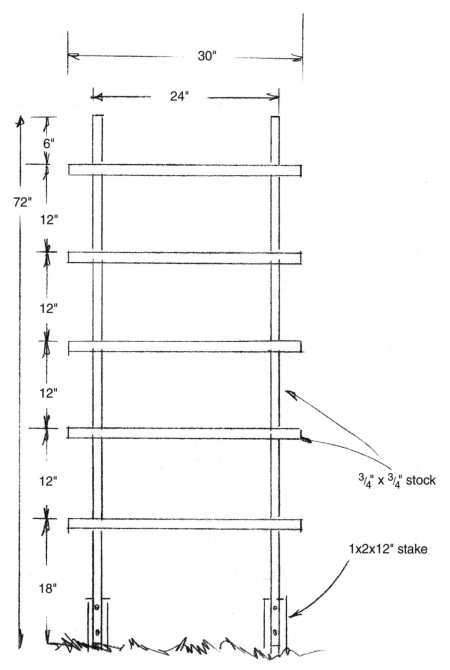

30"

24"

6"

72"

12"

12"

12"

12"

18"

3/4" x 3/4" stock

1x2x12" stake

A straight trellis.

FAN TRELLIS

Designed in the traditional manner, this trellis looks great in a country backyard. It is also fairly easy to make. Again, the first step is to rip the strips to the correct width. Cut the uprights to the proper length. Fasten their bottom ends together with two bolts. Lay the assembly on a smooth flat surface, such as a worktable, and use a wood clamp to clamp the bottom solidly in place. Then clamp the center upright to the worktable

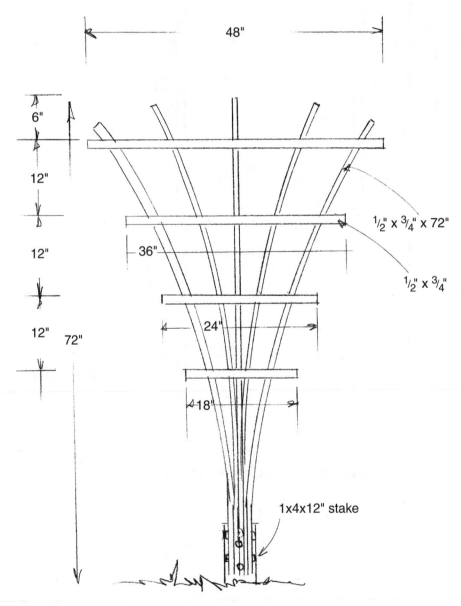

A fan trellis.

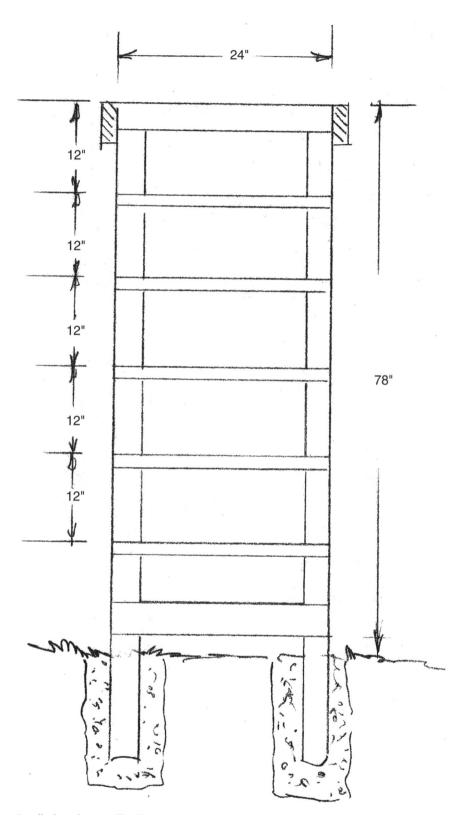

24"

12"

12"

12"

12"

12"

12"

78"

A walk-through rose trellis. (Figure continues on next page.)

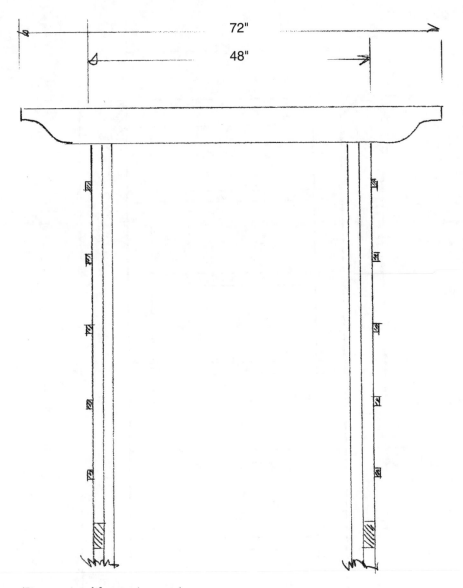

(Figure continued from previous page.)

(Figure continued from previous page.)

as well. Cut the horizontals to the correct lengths. Spread out the two uprights on either side of the center upright to the desired width at the location of the bottom horizontal. Fasten the bottom horizontal in place with self-starting wood screws. Then spread out the outer uprights to their position and fasten the horizontal to them as well. Spread out the uprights to the correct position and install the middle horizontal. Then spread out the uprights further and fasten the top horizontal in place. Cut the 1-×-4-×-12 inch wooden support stake. Drive the stake in place and fasten the trellis to the stake with two bolts.

Materials List

uprights: ½ × ¾ × 72 in., 5 req'd
top horizontal: ½ × ¾ × 48 in., 1 req'd
second horizontal: ½ × ¾ × 36 in., 1 req'd
third horizontal: ½ × ¾ × 24 in., 1 req'd
bottom horizontal: ½ × ¾ × 18 in., 1 req'd
support stake: 1 × 4 × 12 in., 1 req'd
bolts: ¼ × 3 in., 2 req'd

WALK-THROUGH ROSE TRELLIS

Although this is a traditional design for climbing roses, it can be used to support any vining plant. This design utilizes 2-×-4 uprights set in concrete in the ground. Four uprights are required. Make sure you set them square with each other and spaced properly. Once the concrete has set, cut their tops level with each other, starting with the lowest top. Cut the topside supports from 2 × 4s and fasten them in place, making sure they are all level. Then cut the bottom-side supports to length and fasten them in place. Rip 2 × 4s into 2 × 2s for upright blocking and fasten to the outside corners of the upright posts. Rip the side ¾-×-1-inch side horizontals, and then cut to length. Fasten to the side blocking pieces. Cut the top pieces to length and cut the decorative ends using a saber saw. Then fasten the tops in place to the front and back of the posts.

Materials List

uprights: 2 × 4 × 8 ft., 4 req'd
top and bottom supports: 2 × 4 × 24 in., 4 req'd
blocking: 2 × 2 × 65 in., 4 req'd
side horizontals: ¾ × 1 × 24 in., 10 req'd
top pieces: 2 × 6 × 72 in., 2 req'd

CHAPTER 3

BACKYARD TABLES AND BENCHES

WHAT BACKYARD WOULD BE complete without a picnic table for those summer outdoor meals and barbeques? And even a small backyard garden can become a quiet retreat when you add a bench for those times you want to get away from it all and just enjoy a little nature.

CLASSIC PICNIC TABLE

The design for the table shown has been around for many years. It consists of a table and separate benches. The table and benches appear fairly easy to make, but it's important to make sure all angles are cut correctly. You may wish to make up trial end constructions to check all angles. Once you have the angles set, make all cuts on all matching pieces before changing the tool for another step.

Traditional picnic tables and benches are suitable for patios or ponds, decks or picnic shelters. This set is easy to build, if you take your time and get the leg angles right.

Build the table first. The first step is to cut the tabletop pieces to the correct length. Lay them together upside down on a smooth, flat work surface and fasten the

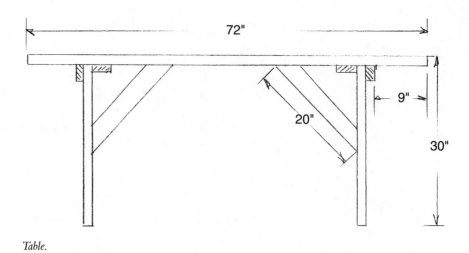

Table.

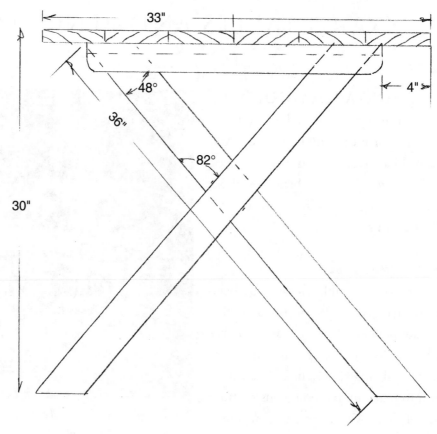

End view of table.

Dado head in a radial arm or table saw is the ideal way to cut the cross-lap joints of the legs.

Fasten legs in place to the inside cleat. The outside cleats will add additional strengthening.

inside cleats down over them with screws, making sure the ends are all square and the pieces are butted tightly together. Then construct one end. The ends of the table and benches are constructed using half-lap, dado joints. A radial arm or table saw with a dado blade is the easiest method of making these joints. After making the cuts, fasten the lapped pieces together with exterior wood screws. Then position the end in place down on the tabletop and against the inside cleats. Fasten in place with wood screws. Cut the outside cleats to length. Round their bottom corners using a band saw, saber saw, or belt sander. Fasten in place with screws into the legs. Cut the leg braces and fasten in place, making sure the leg assembly is square with the tabletop. Repeat with the opposite-end construction. Turn the table upright and drive screws down into the outside cleats and in to the ends of the support cleats.

The outside cleats should have their bottom edges rounded or cut at 45 degrees to remove sharp corners.

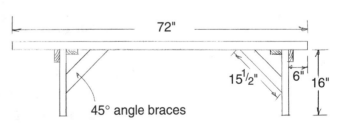

Bench side view.

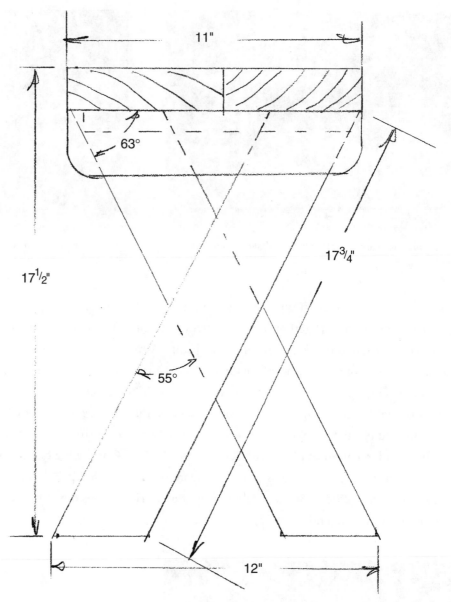

Bench end view.

The benches are constructed in the same manner as the table.

Materials List:

tabletop: ¾ × 6 × 72 in., 6 req'd

table legs: 2 × 4 × 36 in., 4 req'd

table inside cleats: 2 × 4 × 25 in., 2 req'd

table outside cleats: 2 × 4 x 25 in., 2 req'd

support braces: 2 × 4 × 20 in., 2 req'd

bench tops: 2 × 6 × 72 in., 4 req'd

bench legs: 2 × 4 × 17¾ in., 8 req'd

bench inside cleats: 2 × 4 × 10 in., 4 req'd

bench outside cleats: 2 × 4 × 11 in., 4 req'd

bench braces: 2 × 4 × 15½ in., 4 req'd

CLASSIC GARDEN BENCH

The bench shown is a composite of the many garden benches I've seen, and some I've built, over the years. The bench shown is constructed of red cedar that was cut, sawn on a TimberKing band saw mill, and cured from our farm. Other appropriate woods for the project would include redwood, Western white cedar, cypress, and even the hardwoods, such as oak or ash. Because I had some odd-thickness pieces of the red cedar to use up, this was a good project for them. You can, however, utilize standard ¾-inch dimension materials for everything but the legs, which should be a minimum of 3 × 3 inch thickness.

The first step is to cut the legs to the correct length. Then cut the seat support pieces to length. Enlarge the squared drawing for the shape of their tops. Transfer this pattern to the stock and cut to shape using a saber saw or band saw. Attach the end seat support pieces to the insides of the legs. Hold a carpenter's square against the joints and make sure the legs are square with the seat support pieces. (Note: Regardless of the species of material being used, all holes should be predrilled and/or countersunk to prevent splitting out the material and to seat the screw heads

Classic garden bench shown is made of red cedar. It could easily be made of other species to suit your backyard décor.

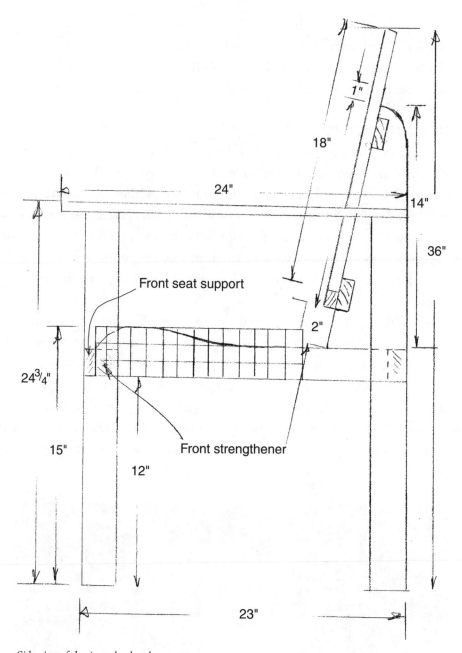

1"

18"

24"

14"

36"

Front seat support

2"

24³/₄"

Front strengthener

15"

12"

23"

Side view of classic garden bench.

below the wood surface. The screws can be left exposed or you may wish to countersink them deeper and cut wood plugs to cover.) Enlarge the squared drawing for the arm rests. Transfer to the stock and cut to shape. Then fasten the armrests down on the tops of the legs.

Cut the front and rear seat supports, ripping them to the correct width and cutting to length. Fasten between the leg assemblies. Then cut the center seat support. The

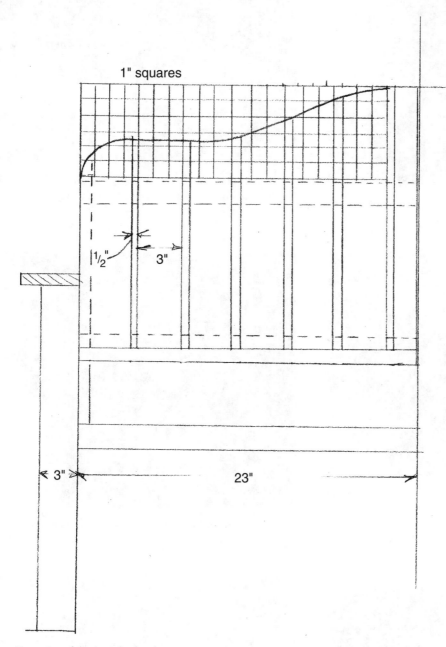

Front view of classic garden bench.

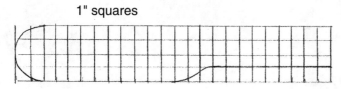

Armrest pattern of classic garden bench.

Trace arm rest pattern onto wood of choice and cut with band saw.

It's very important to make sure the legs are fastened square with the seat supports. Use a carpenter's square to test for squareness.

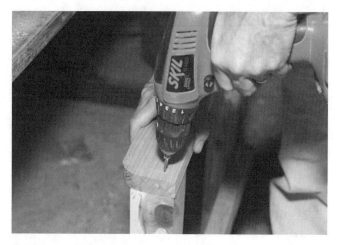

Bench is assembled with screws. The first step is to drill the screw holes and countersink.

Cordless powered drill/driver makes quick work of installing screws.

Seat supports are installed next.

Corner braces are used to brace and strengthen the seat assembly.

Slats are installed over the seat supports following the front curve of the seat supports.

Shown is the basic bench seat frame

center seat support is notched to fit over a front strengthener piece. Cut the strengthener and fit between the leg assemblies, and then fasten the center seat support in place. Cut the 45-degree angle seat braces and install them in place. Then rip the seat slats to the correct widths. Note the first three front slats are 1-inch wide in order to fit over the front curve of the seat supports. The remainder of the slats are 1½ inches wide. Fit the seat boards in place, fastening them down to the seat supports.

Cut the back side supports on a band saw. Cut notches in their front edges for the back slat supports. Rip the slat supports and fit them into the notches in the back side supports. Fasten the side supports in place between the back legs. Cut the slats to length

The backrests are fastened to the upper ends of the legs.

Then the seat slats are placed in position on the seat supports, spacing them properly.

The back slats are cut to the proper shape on a band saw and installed on the back slat supports.

and width and then cut the shaped upper ends on a band saw. Install the slats over the slat supports, spacing them ½ inch apart. It's a good idea to mark all slat locations before installing any slats. If the spaces are not exactly even, you can shift slightly before fastening the slats in place.

Add a coat or two of exterior finish, and you're ready to enjoy a classic garden bench.

Materials List

legs: 3 × 3 × 24 in., 4 req'd

seat supports: 1½ × 3 × 20¾ in., 3 req'd

arms: ¾ × 4 × 24 in., 2 req'd

back seat support: 1½ × 3 × 46 in., 1 req'd

front seat strengthener: 1½ × 1½ × 46 in., 1 req'd

seat corner braces: 1½ × 3 × 9 in., 4 req'd

front seat slats: ¾ × 1 × 46 in., 3 req'd

seat slats: ¾ × 1½ × 46 in., 8 req'd

seat back side supports: ¾ × 5 × 14 in., 2 req'd

back slat supports: ¾ × 2 × 46 in., 2 req'd

back slats: ¾ × 3 × 18 in., 13 req'd

bottom back slat support: ¾ × 1 × 46 in., 1 req'd

SLAB BENCHES

Some of the most novel backyard décor includes benches made of wood slabs. In the olden days, of necessity, many furniture items were made of slabs and saplings. It's a great way these days to utilize sawmill slabs as well as saplings taken during woodlot thinning operations to build camp- or lodge-style furniture. This easy-to-make furniture is extremely sturdy in addition to adding a "rustic" flavor to the backyard.

If you have a woodlot, you probably have plenty of materials for rustic furniture. Most woodlots benefit from thinning trees, removing dead trees, and other timber management practices. With a chain saw and portable bandsaw mill, such as the TimberKing, you can acquire all types of building materials. If you don't have a woodlot, slabs are often free for the asking at sawmills, and tree trimmings or branches may be available from dealers in cordwood.

The type of woods will vary with availability and locality and may range from oak to cedar to pine to redwood, birch, and cypress. Furniture that is to be left outdoors should be made of redwood, cedar, oak, or cypress.

For most construction you'll need slabs at least 4 feet long and 12 to 18 inches wide. These slabs should be from 3 to 6 inches thick at their thickest part. With some

Furniture such as this wood slab and sapling bench can create a rustic feel to any backyard décor.

Slabs, or the waste from sawmills, are used to create the bench.

species, the bark may be left on, especially for outdoor furniture. Some species tend to shed their bark and it's best to remove it. Cedar is a good example of a wood that looks best with the bark removed.

You will also need saplings for the legs. Again, you'll have to use wood that is readily available locally. The saplings should range from 1 to 3 inches in diameter for benches and tables. Just about any sapling wood will do. They also don't have to match the wood used for the slabs and the bark can be left on or removed from the legs as well.

You really don't need a lot of tools for this project; the furniture can be constructed with simple hand tools. You may want to use a chain saw for cutting trees and saplings as well as for faster cutting of pieces to length. A hand crosscut saw or bucksaw can also be used for cutting the pieces to length. A brace and bits (including an expansive bit), drawknife, spokeshave, hammer or mallet, and jack will build most projects. If you get into large-scale furniture production there are also powered tenoning tools that can be used to cut the round tenons quickly and easily on the ends of the legs as well as various other power tools to make the jobs easier.

The sawn surface of the slabs may be quite rough, especially if sawn on large circular saw mills. Bandsaw mills, on the other hand, leave a quite smooth surface. Rough surfaces may need to be smoothed up. The amount of smoothness depends on your desires. The surfaces can be smoothed with the jackplane, or a powered belt sander can be used for initial smoothing, followed by finish sanders if you prefer an extremely smooth surface. The ends should also be smoothed up. The edges and corners should be smoothed and rounded. Then inspect the entire piece for any splinters or sharp edges. Some extremely rough bark may also need to be smoothed slightly with the drawknife or spokeshave. Try to use sapling sections without knots or bumps. If they do have knots or bumps, cut them flush or smooth them up. Inspect the saplings to make sure there are no sharp bumps or knots.

At this point you're ready to begin construction. Determine the length of the legs. Remember in this type of furniture, the legs are usually placed at an angle and this requires slightly longer lengths. The next step is to

The legs are cut to length from saplings, and then tenons cut on the legs using a tenoning jig from Woodcraft Supply in a portable electric drill.

Round the edges of the bench with a drawknife.

Holes are bored at an angle with a Forstner bit and portable electric drill or brace and bit.

determine the diameter of the tenons. This will usually be just slightly smaller than the outside diameter or bark if it is left on. A 1-inch diameter is a good starting point. Once you've decided on the diameter, set the expansive bit to the correct size and bore the holes for the legs. Make sure to keep the angles the same for all four legs. The easiest way of doing this is with an angle-boring jig. This allows you to assure correct and consistent angles on all holes. The angle should be between 15 and 20 degrees in two directions. Using the drawknife, and with the leg clamped in a vise or other type of clamp, shape the end of the leg into a round tenon that will fit snugly into the hole.

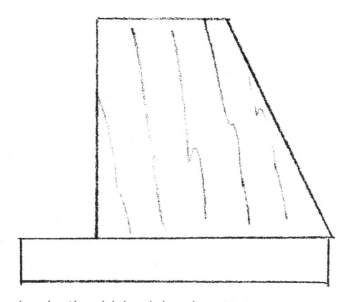

An angle guide can help keep the leg angles consistent.

The ends of the tenon and wedges are cut flush with the bench top.

Slots are cut in the top of the tenons and the tenons driven into the holes. Wedges are then cut to fit into the slots and driven in place.

Tenons are quickly and easily cut with a tenon-making tool from Woodcraft Supply. The tool fits in a portable electric drill.

Tenons may be fastened in place in one of three ways. If the wood is seasoned, which it rarely is in this type of construction, you can glue the tenons in place. Or you can drive a nail in at an angle to hold the tenons. The more traditional and best method, however, is to anchor the tenons in place with a wedge. This can be with a concealed or blind wedge, or the wedge can be exposed. The exposed method also allows you to retighten the tenons should they come loose. To create a blind wedge, try-fit the tenon in place. It should be snug, but not too tight. Saw a slot in the top of the tenon and start a thin and short wedge in place. Then insert the tenon-with-wedge in place and use the mallet or hammer to drive it securely in place. A better method is the open tenon. In this case the hole for the tenon is bored all the way through the slab. The tenon is cut long enough so about ½ inch protrudes through the top of the slab. A slot is cut in the top of the tenon, and the tenon driven in place in the hole. A wedge is then driven in from the top of the slab. Once the leg is wedged tightly in place, the end of the tenon and wedge are cut off flush with the top of the slab. The slab is then sanded or planed to smooth the joints. Because most of this type of furniture is made of green wood, it will eventually shrink and the legs become loose. To retighten, simply drive in another wedge or a larger wedge. On thick slabs, a pin can be used to hold the tenons in place.

Once the bench or stool is assembled, place it on a flat, smooth surface. You'll discover it probably doesn't sit flat. Use small pieces of wood to wedge the shorter legs until the furniture piece sits flat and level. Mark the amount needed to be removed from a leg or legs to create a level surface. Mark all around the leg so you can cut the leg flat or you'll end up continually cutting. With the piece on its side, saw the legs to the correct length.

Once you construct a simple bench or stool, you'll probably wish to tackle a few projects that are more complicated. These can include benches and chairs with backs and arms on them. The same basic construction methods are used. Backs are usually held in place with wooden pins or nails.

You can also make tables in the same manner. It usually requires several slabs for the top or you may be able to acquire some planks. If you have a portable sawmill, you can make the plank tables quite easily.

BACKYARD PLAYING

Like cookies and ice cream, kids and backyards go hand in hand. You can make your backyard even more kid-oriented with the projects in this chapter, including a tree fort, playhouse, and sandboxes.

CHAPTER 1

TREE FORT

KIDS LOVE TREE HOUSES. Kids love forts. Kids love slides and other activity sets. The tree fort shown combines all of those features and then some.

Nailing or bolting into trees to construct tree houses, however, is not without problems and dangers. Fasteners can come loose, creating dangerous situations. Trees can also grow around the fasteners and some trees can expand fast enough to cause a structural problem. Enough metal in trees can also affect their health, creating places for rot to start, and eventually killing the tree. The tree fort shown is freestanding; it's simply built *around* a tree. This provides the tree-house/fort for play, but doesn't harm the tree. The tree, however, still provides some of the excitement, as well as shade for playtime. In addition to the "fort" on top as shown, there is a slide, "monkey bars," and a swing set. The swing set and slide were bought at a local building supply dealer. A wide selection of these play items are available. You can add or subtract play items as desired or to suit the ages of your children or grandchildren.

A tree fort combines the mystery of a fort and the shade of a tree with the fun of a play set.

The first prerequisite is to choose the right tree. Fruit trees or nut trees that may drop their harvest into and onto the tree fort should be avoided—for obvious reasons. Also avoid evergreens, such as cedar, or other trees that may

The set shown features a purchased slide.

It also features a purchased swing set and trapeze bar.

Monkey bars and ladder are home constructed.

A temporary 2-x-4 bottom frame is used to lay out the project and locate the position of the four corner posts. It must be square.

exude sap, as well as those that have sharp stickers. The tree should also be healthy without an excess of dead limbs. Any dead or dying limbs must be removed before construction. Especially examine the top of the tree to make sure there are no openings indicating a rotting interior. Trim back any limbs necessary for safe construction as well as safe usage.

It's important to use long-lasting materials such as California redwood or Wolmanized Natural Select for this project. See the chapter on Materials for more information on outdoor-use woods.

The first step in construction is to lay out the fort. You can follow the general measurements shown, or change the measurements to suit your particular tree and situation. In most constructions of this type, stakes are driven into the ground at the corners, then diagonal measurements taken to create a "square" project. Since this isn't possible with a tree protruding through the center of the project, a temporary "box" is constructed, the size of the fort bottom, using 2 × 4s. Scrape the ground around the tree to level the area somewhat. Then assemble the box frame using duplex or double-headed nails or galvanized nails driven only partially in place. Move the box frame around until you're satisfied with the general location in relation to the tree trunk. Stand 2 × 4s in each corner and make sure no limbs will protrude through the top of

It should also be level and temporarily staked in place.

The support poles are located in each corner. Mark for the locations and dig the holes.

Set the poles in the holes and make sure they are plumb. Anchor the bottom support frame to each pole.

The Craftsman Smart Tool Plus Level makes an easy job of leveling and plumbing all portions of the project.

the fort construction and that the entire construction will be properly located. Then use a carpenter's square to square up all corners. Drive a stake in each corner. The outside edges of the stakes will be the outside edges of the uprights. Shift the frame slightly so it isn't in the way, and then dig the holes for the four corner uprights in these locations. Reposition the frame in place, checking to make sure the holes extend past the outside edges for the concrete. Again, check to make sure the frame is square. Stake the frame in place with stakes driven around the outside edges. Stand a corner pole in place and, with its sides against the inside corners of the bottom frame, plumb the pole in both ways with a 4-foot level. Temporarily fasten the frame to the pole with duplex nails. Use temporary braces on two sides of the poles to hold them in place. Then mix Sakrete or other pre-mixed concrete and fill in the hole around the pole. Make sure the concrete doesn't protrude above ground level or have sharp edges that can be dangerous when it sets up. Do the remaining upright poles for the fort in the same manner and allow all to set. Note: after construction, remove the temporary bottom frame.

If using a purchased slide, such as the unit shown from Swing-n-Slide, the floor height will be determined by the slide.

Make sure all posts are braced plumb.

Pre-mixed bagged concrete such as Sakrete is mixed and poured around the posts.

The 10-foot slide shown resulted in a floor height of 66 inches on the ground situation shown. This can vary according to the specific slide. If you don't use a slide, or a different slide, you can place the floor height as desired or to match the slide instructions. It's extremely important to carefully follow all installation and safety instructions with the slide you purchase.

Make sure the concrete does not protrude above the ground level and that the surface is smooth and rounded.

Once the poles have set, fasten the joist headers and braces in place with lag bolts.

Once all the poles have thoroughly set, and the floor height is established, temporarily tack the floor joist headers outside the poles, making sure the headers are level as you go around the fort. Once all are leveled in place, fasten the floor joist headers with lag screws and washers. Cut 45-degree angle braces and fasten them to each corner, again with lag screws and washers. Using joist hangers, cut, fit, and install the floor joists. Note these joists go "around" the tree and should be positioned about 1 to 2 inches from the tree in all directions to allow for tree growth and tree sway in windstorms (depending on the tree species and trunk diameter). Floor joists are actually "boxed" to go around the tree. On the unit shown three joists were used longitudinally, with two short stretcher joists spaced between.

With the joists in place, cut and install the ¾-inch decking boards for the floor. Use hot-dipped galvanized or coated decking screws and make sure the heads are slightly countersunk below the wood surface. Make sure the flooring does not protrude out past the outside edges of the joist headers. Don't leave more than 1 inch of space between the deck board ends and the tree to prevent a child from getting a foot caught. With the flooring in place, install the slide in the center of one side, making sure it is installed according to manufacturer's instructions.

Cut the upright rail supports on either side of the slide opening to the correct height. Cut the top railings for the slide side. Fasten the uprights in place with 4-inch angle irons on their bottom back edges. Fasten the 2-×-4 top rails to the posts and uprights, making sure they are level. Two sides of the unit shown have solid "fort" sides.

The floor is made from ¾ decking. It must be notched to fit around the posts.

One is also used to anchor the swing set. Fasten these two top railings in place to the upright posts, again making sure they are level.

Next, the monkey bar assembly is constructed in the center of another fort side. This assembly consists of two posts set in concrete, two 2 × 6s used as horizontal supports and two 2 × 6s as vertical ladder supports. Determine the length of the vertical ladder supports. The ladder supports on this model are 8 feet in length. Their bottom ends are anchored to 4-×-4 "stakes" set in concrete. Their top corners are rounded using a saber saw. Lay the vertical ladder supports side by side and mark the locations of the ladder rungs. Drill holes through the 2 × 6s using a spade bit. You might want to try the new Bosch RapidFeed Spade Bits. They have a patent-pending tip similar to the screw tip of an auger bit. This design helps pull the bit through the wood, greatly reducing the amount of force and effort needed while feeding the bit through. Make sure to back up the work piece so it doesn't splinter when the bit comes through on the back side. Or you can partially drill through one side, then turn and drill from the opposite side.

Cut the closest pole to the lengths needed for the rungs and drive them into the holes in the uprights. Use a deck screw driven

The floor is attached with decking screws. It must also be cut to fit around the tree.

The posts are located for the monkey bars and swings. Holes are dug and concrete used to secure the posts.

Construct the monkey bar. The first step is to round the ends of both the vertical and horizontal supports that attach to the fort.

Holes for monkey bars and swing chain hangers can be bored with a spade bit.

from the backside into each rung to secure the rungs. Anchor the ladder in place with lag screws driven from the back through the upper rail. Again, the lower ends are anchored to short 4-×-4 stakes set in concrete.

Cut, bore the holes, and construct the horizontal monkey bar assembly in the same manner. The corners of the fort-ends of these horizontals are also rounded. Determine the location of the monkey bar end support posts. Measure directly out from the ladder support pieces and then measure from each corner of the fort support posts. Shift the location of the two posts until they are equally spaced from each fort post. Dig the holes, set the support posts in place with concrete, making sure they are plumb, and allow them to set up. Use a long straightedge and level to mark the location of the level height from the fort support ends to the location

The Bosch RapidFeed Spade Bit features a screw tip for rapid boring.

Forstner bits can also be used for this chore. Make sure the workpiece is backed up to prevent splintering out the back.

on the outer support posts. Cut them to this height and then fasten the monkey bar assembly in place to the ladder assembly and the two posts using lag screws through the outer ends to the support posts and carriage bolts on the fort end. Note these bolt heads must be driven in so that their rounded edges are on the inside of the horizontals and provide no sharp edges. Construct the upper rails and rail supports on that side in the same manner as for the slide side.

The swing side of the fort has a post located in the center of one side of the fort and anchored to the top rail and floor joist header. The bottom end is set in concrete. The outer end of the swing assembly also utilizes a post set in concrete. Measure from each fort corner post to position the "outrigger" posts properly. Note these posts must be set at least 3 feet in the ground. The swing top beam consists of a 4 × 6 across the ends of the two posts. Use a straight edge and 4-foot level to mark a level line across the tops of the posts and cut them to the same height. Metal joining brackets are used to initially anchor the top beam in place. Then 2-×-4 "strengtheners" are fastened on both sides of both

Bolt the monkey bars assembly and swing supports in place.

Install the hanging swing and trapeze bar as per the manufacturer's instructions.

posts and 2 × 6s on the post ends for additional strength. Lag bolts are used for these. The swing and the trapeze bar for the unit shown were then fastened in place. Again, make sure you follow all safety rules for installation of the play equipment.

The next step is to cut the fort sides from ¾ decking material. Note they are spaced 3 inches apart. They are anchored to the joist headers and the top rails using brass decking screws. Cut the corner posts off a couple of inches above the corner side

Assemble the upper rails and supports and nail on the sides.

Install the hanging swing and trapeze bar as per the manufacturer's instructions.

pieces and cut their edges at a 45-degree angle. Last step is to bore a hole in each corner block and install the pennants for "fort décor."

With the project completed, go over the entire surface sanding all sharp edges. Round all corners as needed and de-burr any metal edges.

Before children are allowed to play on the unit, proper shock absorbing materials must be installed. The Consumer Product Safety Commission suggests the following

Cut 45-degree edges on all exposed posts, sand all edges, round all corners, and de-burr all metal.

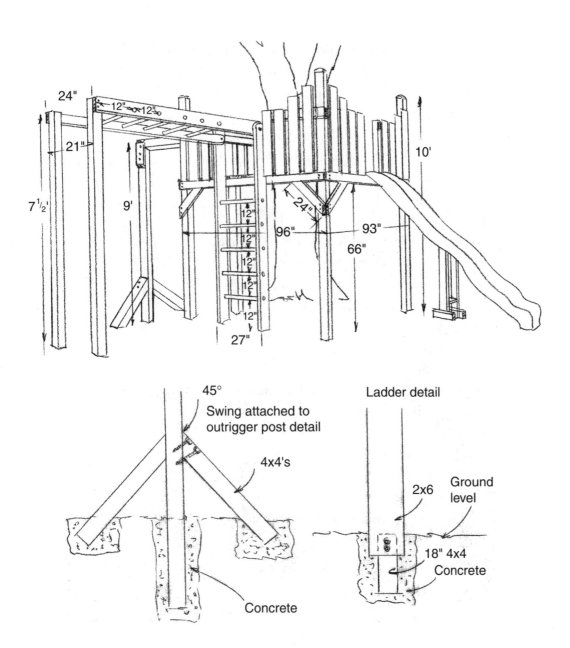

45°
Swing attached to
outrigger post detail

4x4's

Concrete

Ladder detail

2x6

Ground
level

18" 4x4
Concrete

materials and depths: wood mulch, 9 inches; double-shredded bark mulch, 9 inches; uniform wood chips, 12 inches; fine sand, 12 inches; fine gravel, 12 inches.

For a really unusual backyard, build a tree fort. Your kids and grandkids will love you for it.

Materials List

fort posts: 4 × 4 × 12 ft., 4 req'd

monkey-bar posts: 4 × 4 × 10 ft., 2 req'd

swing set posts: 4 × 4 × 12 ft., 2 req'd

swing set top beam: 4 × 6 × 10 ft., 1 req'd

side swing set post strengtheners: 2 × 4 × 12 in., 4 req'd

end swing set post strengtheners: 2 × 6 × 12 in., 2 req'd

floor joist headers: 2 × 4 × 8 ft., 4 req'd

floor joists: 2 × 4 × 8 ft., 3 req'd

stretcher joists: 2 × 4 × 3 ft. (cut to fit), 2 req'd

floor joist braces: 2 × 4 × 24 in., 8 req'd

flooring: ¾ decking, 17 req'd

top rails: 2 × 4 × 8 ft., 4 req'd

top upright rail supports: 2 × 4 × 30 in., 4 req'd

monkey bar ladder verticals: 2 × 6 × 8 ft., 2 req'd

monkey bar horizontals: 2 × 6 × 8 ft., 2 req'd

monkey bars: 1¼-in. closet pole, 24 in., 11 req'd

siding: ¾ decking, 31 in., 21 req'd

siding: ¾ decking, 36 in., 8 req'd

siding: ¾ decking, 40 in., 8 req'd

lag bolts: with washers ⅜ × 3 in., 38 req'd

carriage bolts: ⅜ × 4 in. with washers and nuts, 2 req'd

brass or coated deck screws

galvanized nails

angle irons: 4 in., 8 req'd

metal post brackets: 2 req'd

concrete for posts

play set equipment (swings, slide, etc.), as desired.

CHAPTER 2

PLAYHOUSE

THE BUILDING SHOWN IS extremely versatile. Constructed as a playhouse, it can also act as a garden shed. The woman who owns this house now uses it to store tack for her Arabian show horses. The building is portable and sits on concrete blocks, as does the decorative porch. Construction is basic house building in a miniature way. The building is covered with Louisiana Pacific Smart Panels with metal corner trim. A front dormer, window shutters, and window box, as well as a fake chimney, add to the charm. Two windows are located in the front with one in the back. Other doors and windows could be added to suit.

The building sits on a "box" floor frame, supported on concrete blocks. The building could also be constructed on skids if desired, which would make the building more portable. The first step is to build a basic box frame of 2-×-6 headers. Position this on the concrete blocks and make sure it is square and level. Then add the 2-×-6 floor joists between the front and back pieces of the frame. Again, make sure the assembly is square. Fasten ¾-inch plywood flooring down over the frame.

You're now ready for the wall framing. Frame up one end wall. Blocking should be installed in the ends in order to provide a corner for finishing off the interior.

This versatile building can serve as a playhouse, garden shed, or storage building. This particular building has been used as all three. It currently stores horse tack and feed.

The shuttered front windows and planting boxes for flowers make this a very decorative backyard structure.

Stand up the end wall in place on the wooden floor and plumb. Brace it with 2 × 4s nailed into the outside ends and to the floor framing. Nail the floor plate in place with nails through the floor and into the outside floor headers. Construct and erect the opposite end wall. Construct the back wall and erect it in the same manner between the end walls, and then construct the front wall and erect it between the end walls. Add doors and windows to the back and side walls to suit. Make sure all walls are plumb and the corners meet properly and then fasten the corners together. Add the tie plates over the walls to lock the corners together. Cut away the bottom plate for the door openings.

Build the end-to-end rafter system, cutting the rafters to the correct shape with the bird's mouth notch to hold them in place on the tie plates. Fasten the rafters to the ridge board and to the tie plates. Add collar ties to strengthen the rafters. When you reach the location of the dormer ends, build the front rafter assembly of the dormer, attaching a ridge board between the two front rafters and the end-to-end ridge board. Then cut the valley rafters to fit from

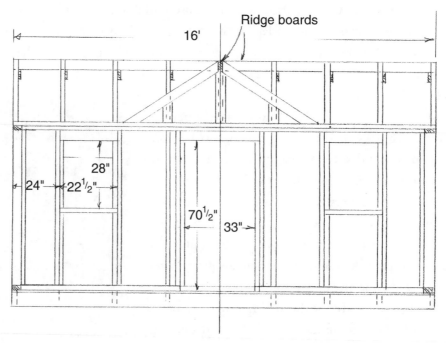

Playhouse front view.

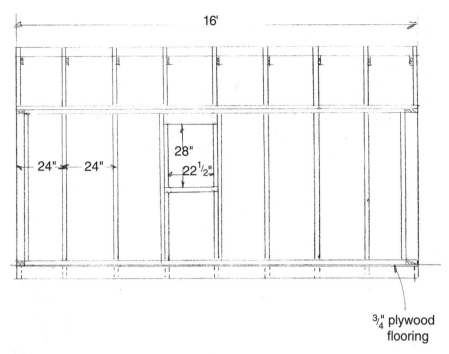

16'

24" 24"

28"

22 1/2"

3/4" plywood
flooring

Playhouse back view.

the main ridge board, abutting into the sides of the dormer ridge board and down on the tie plate and against the front dormer rafters. Then cut the jack rafters to fit between the valley and ridge rafters. Although the building is fairly small, creating the dormer will probably take a bit of fiddling, cutting, and recutting the dormer rafters until you get the correct angles and lengths. The backside end-to-end rafters are cut and installed to match the front rafters. Nailing blocks must be installed on the ends and the front of the dormer to fasten the siding in place.

With the rafters installed, cut the front and back soffit pieces and fasten to the ends of the rafters. Cut the siding and install it. Cut out the door, window, and vent openings after the siding has been installed. Metal corner strips finish off the siding. Add the matching drip edge and then shingle the roof. After the roof has been shingled the faux chimney is made. It is then fastened down over the shingles with screws through cleats from the inside. A top is then added to prevent rainwater from coming in and collecting.

Install the vents, fasten the windows in place, and fasten the shutters to the sides of the windows. Make the window flower boxes and fasten below the windows. The door is constructed of an interior framework of 1 x 4s and the cut-out door siding piece installed over the framework. The door is hinged to 1-×-2 trim pieces fastened on both sides and a matching piece installed over the top.

The miniature deck is then created by building a 2-×-4 framework with 2-×-4 floor joists. The deck is also supported on concrete blocks. Decking boards are fastened down on the deck frame, making sure the frame is square. Cut the deck posts to the

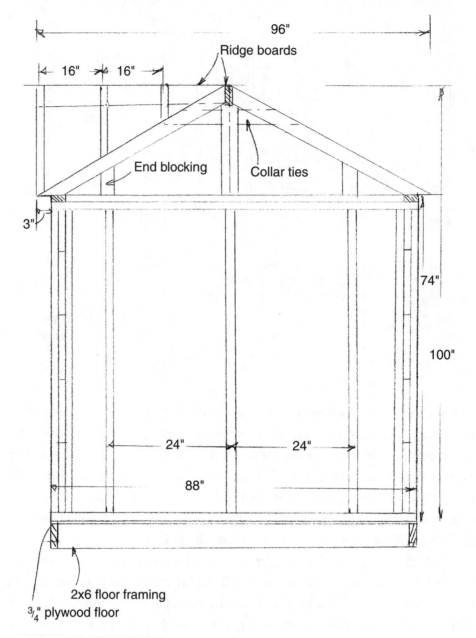

96"

Ridge boards

16" 16"

End blocking

Collar ties

3"

74"

100"

24" 24"

88"

2x6 floor framing

3/4" plywood floor

Playhouse end view.

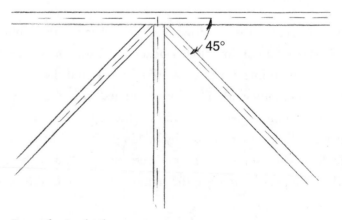

45°

Dormer framing detail.

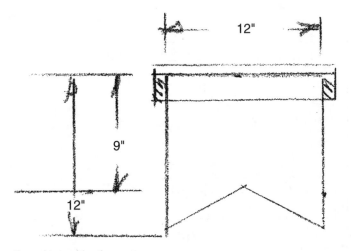

Faux chimney detail.

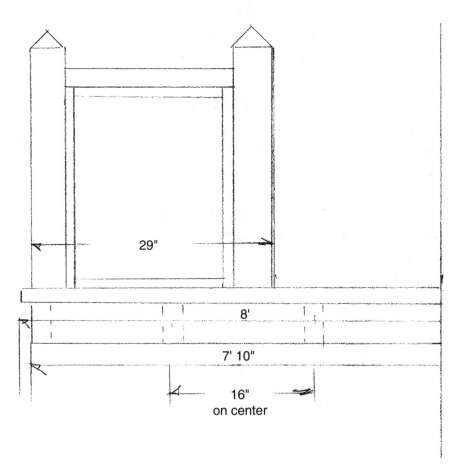

Front view deck.

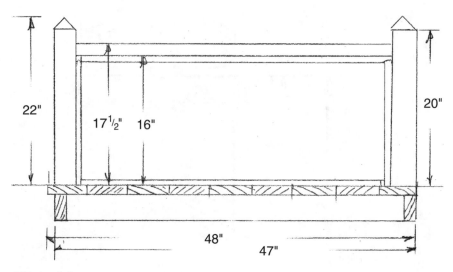

Side view deck.

correct length and make 45-degree angle cuts in their top ends to create the pointed tops. Toenail the posts in place. Then add the outside top and side cleats to the posts. Cut the lattice panels to fit against the cleats and add the inside bottom and side cleats. Nail the "railing" down over the ends of the side cleats.

Materials List:
front and back headers: 2 × 6 in. × 16 ft., 2 req'd
end headers: 2 × 6 in. × 8 ft., cut to fit, 2 req'd
floor joists: 2 × 6 in. × 8 ft., cut to fit, 7 req'd
flooring: ¾ in. × 4 × 8 ft. plywood, 4 req'd
wall studs: 2 × 4 in. × 8 ft., 36 req'd
window and door headers: 2 × 4 in. × 10 ft., 2 req'd
ridge board: 2 × 4 in. × 16 ft., 1 req'd
rafters: 2 × 4 in. × 4 ft., 18 req'd
collar ties: 2 × 4 × 24 in., 9 req'd
dormer ridge board: 2 × 4 in. × 4 ft., 1 req'd
dormer rafters: 2 × 4 × 48 in., 6 req'd
valley rafters: 2 × 4 × 6 in., 2 req'd
front and end blocking: 2 × 4 × 6 in., 9 req'd
siding: ¾ × 4 in. × 8 ft., 15 req'd
roof sheathing: ½ × 4 in. × 8 ft., 9 req'd
shingles: 3 square req'd
drip edge: 70 ft. req'd

windows: 22½ × 28 in., 3 req'd

shutters: 3 pair req'd

soffit: 1 × 3, 32 ft. req'd

metal corner trim (also on chimney corners): 350 ft. req'd

Z-channel: 2 ft. req'd

chimney framing and cap trim: 1 × 2 in. × 12 ft., 1 req'd

door trim: 1 × 2 in. × 15 ft., 1 req'd

doorframe: 1 × 4 in. × 18 ft., cut to fit, 1 req'd

vents: 2 req'd

deck headers, sides: 2 × 4 × 47 in., 2 req'd

deck headers, front and back: 2 × 4 ft. × 8 ft., 2 req'd

deck floor joists: 2 × 4 × 47 in., 5 req'd

deck top: ¾ × 5½ in. × 8 ft., 9 req'd

deck posts: 4 × 4 × 22 in., 6 req'd

deck railing, side: 2 × 4 × 40 in., 2 req'd

deck railing, front: 2 × 4 × 22 in., 2 req'd

lattice: 4 × 8 ft., 1 req'd

lattice cleats: ¾ × ¾ in. × 75 ft. req'd

SANDBOXES BIG AND SMALL

Sandboxes don't have to be elaborate to be enjoyed. But, they do have to be sturdy. Sandboxes should, if possible, be located in the shade or out of the direct sun and the area for the sandbox should be scraped level. Since neither of these boxes has a bottom, it's a good idea to place a grass barrier down first. Following are two simple boxes, one small, one larger.

SMALL SANDBOX

Although the sandbox shown is only 5 feet square, it's fairly deep, so it can hold quite a bit of sand for little "excavators." First step is to cut the 2 × 6s to the correct length. Then fasten the cleats flush to the "inside" edges of the sides. A center cleat should also be fastened to hold the centers of the boards together.

Fasten the other two sides together with the end cleats extending so they can cover the ends of the first two sides. Fasten all together with brass deck screws.

Position one "short" side in place with the joining side in place (at the location of the box). Fasten the overlapping joining side with brass screws

Although relatively small, this sandbox is fairly deep to help contain the sand. Corner supports also act as seat boards.

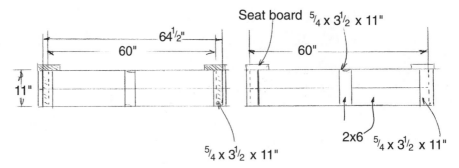

Small sandbox.

into the abutting end of the other side. Fasten the opposite "short" side in place in the same manner. Then finally fasten the opposite "long" side in place.

Cut the 45-degree angle seat boards for the corners. These seat boards also act as "braces" to hold the box square. Use a carpenter's square to square up the box, and then install the seat board/braces down over the top edges of the sides at the corners with brass wood screws. Finally, use a hand plane or sander to make sure all sharp edges and corners are well rounded.

Materials List
sides: 2 × 6 × 60 ft., 8 req'd
corner blocks: 1 × 4 × 11 in., 8 req'd

The corner blocks are used to fasten the sandbox corners together.

Seat boards also provide additional strength at each corner.

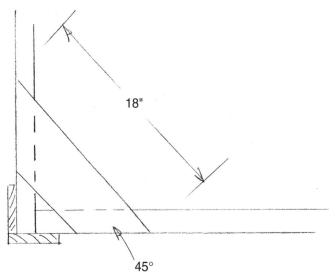

Small sandbox corner detail.

center braces: 1 × 4 × 11 in., 4 req'd

seat boards: 2 × 6 × 18 in., 4 req'd

LARGE SANDBOX

Actually there are no limits to the size this sandbox can be constructed, because it's made out of landscaping timbers. The box shown is made of 8-foot long timbers. First step is to cut the four shorter timbers to a length less the width of two timbers. Then lay the bottom timbers in position on the ground and in the location of the sandbox.

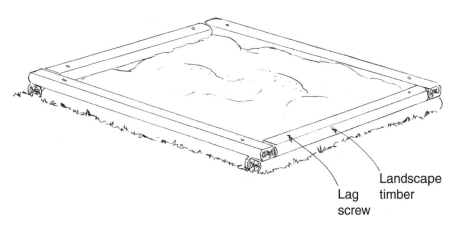

One of the simplest sandboxes can be made using landscaping timbers. Stack the timbers log-style and fasten together with lag screws.

Use a carpenter's square to make sure the timbers are laid out square. It's also a good idea to create a fairly level surface for the timbers to rest on. Scrape away any turf and remove rocks and other debris.

Position the second or upper row of timbers in place over the first. Anchor the timbers in the top layer with lag screws down into the bottom timbers. Countersink the heads and use flat washers under the bolt heads.

Materials List
landscape timbers, length to suit: 8 req'd
lag screws: ⅜ × 6 in., 8 req'd

BACKYARD SHELTERS

Adding shelters to your backyard can not only provide enjoyable, sheltered areas for work and play, but they can also increase the value of your property. A picnic shelter, screened-in porch, and carport all offer weather and sun protection.

CHAPTER 1

SCREENED-IN PORCH

AHHHH, THE ROMANCE OF A screened-in porch—lemonade and cool comfort for those hot summer days and a hammock or chaise lounge for slumbering those warm nights away. And all outside—where you can still enjoy Mother Nature without the hassle of insects. A screened-in porch can not only add to the enjoyment of your home, but to its value as well. A screened-in porch can also be constructed in three phases. Many homeowners have started with a patio, added a roof, and then ended up screening in a porch. The porch shown is a prime example of building in phases over a period of time. Or the project can be done as one from beginning to end.

Note: Regardless of whether adding an enclosure to a roofed area or building from start, in many instances you will be required to provide a building plan for any home addition to a local building authority. You may also be required to obtain a building permit.

SUPPORT

Regardless, the first step is to create a solid base for the construction of the porch. In some instances decks may be utilized. In this case, the area of the deck with the porch must be floored over with a solid material to keep the insects from coming up through the cracks in the deck. Additional support must also be placed under the deck to support the additional weight of the porch, as well as any snow that may accumulate on its

A screened-in porch provides a comfortable, shady, insect-free spot for snoozing, reading, eating, or just enjoying your backyard.

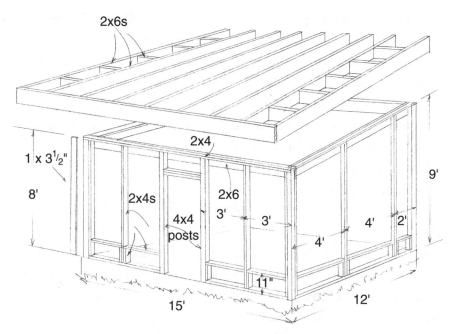

2x6s

1 x 3½"

8'

2x4

2x4s

4x4 posts

2x6

3'

3'

4'

4'

4'

2'

9'

11"

15'

12'

Exploded view of porch.

roof in northern climates. In many instances, however, the porch will be constructed on a concrete or other type of solid patio. The ideal is to pour a concrete slab for the porch, which can then be further embellished with a slate or quarry tile floor. A screened-in porch will have to handle the elements, so make sure all materials used are manufactured for exterior use.

If using a poured concrete slab or other solid surface, make sure there is proper water drainage away from the house because water will get into the porch during storms. Most builders consider ¼ inch per foot the proper slope for a concrete patio. For a 12-foot porch, this would be 3 inches—and this is too much for a porch constructed on a slab. For the porch shown, a pitch of 1 inch for the 12-foot length was used. This doesn't hamper construction quite as much as the sharper pitch, but still allows water drainage.

The slab must be laid out and formed. If you do not have experience in or the tools for concrete work, you may wish to have a contractor do this portion. Pouring a slab of the size shown is do-able for many do-it-yourselfers, if time is taken in laying out the project so that it is square and formed to the proper pitch. Concrete tools are available at many rental stores. Do not attempt, however, to mix the concrete for this project. You will need to purchase bulk concrete. Make sure the slab is well reinforced and a footing is poured around the edge. The footing should be sized to match your geological location. Check with local concrete dealers as to the size and depth. After forming and before pouring, place a layer of gravel down, followed by welded wire reinforcing. Pour the concrete, level it off with a drag, and trowel it smooth. You can hand-trowel, but a power trowel speeds the work and these can also be rented. If building a screened-in porch on a new slab, place anchor bolts around the perimeter in locations for the bottom plate. The plates can then be bolted to the slab to anchor the porch in place. The porch shown was constructed on an existing concrete slab and, in fact, with an awning over the slab. The structure was simply framed in and screened. In this case, the lower plates were anchored in place with a rented concrete gun that shoots anchors through the plates into the concrete.

FRAMING

In the case shown, one corner post was already in existence, but it was partially rotted. A garage formed another side of the porch area. The roof was jacked up slightly and propped in place. The old post was removed, a 2-×-4 top plate positioned in place, and new corner posts inserted under it. Then the door-side posts were installed as well as the opposite corner post. The roof was then lowered slowly in place and the posts anchored to the top plate with 3½-inch exterior wood screws "toe-nailed" through the sides of the posts into the top plate.

If constructing a totally new screened-in porch without the roof already in place, construct the front wall with a bottom and top plate, the 4-×-4 posts, 2-×-4 "studs" and the blocking for the lower framing. Stand the wall upright, make sure it is plumb, and

Craftsman lightweight 3½-inch magnesium framing nailer makes quick and accurate work of constructing the porch framing.

then brace it in place. Construct the side walls, stand them up, and anchor them to the outside wall. Or you can erect the posts, plumb them, and add the 2-×-4 framing and blocking. Cut a 2-×-6 inside "plate" and fasten it inside the front wall and flush with the top edge of the plate. This adds strength to the front support, or you can use a double-top front plate. Then cut an inside support plate for each side and anchor it as well.

If constructing a roof, as opposed to screening in a roofed porch, fasten a sill plate to the house between the two side walls and flush with their top edges. The rafters can then be positioned down on top of this. Joist hangers can also be used to help anchor the house ends of the rafters in place. In many instances, the roof pitch will match that of the house. In some cases, such as the one shown, the roof pitch is much shallower, however. Make sure the pitch is correct for your area and snow load. Again, check with local authorities. For the more shallow-pitched porch roofs, 2-×-6 rafters are suggested. Extend the roof out a foot past the walls. Use blocking on the side to anchor the hanging rafters. A fascia board is fastened to the front edges of the front rafters and to the sides.

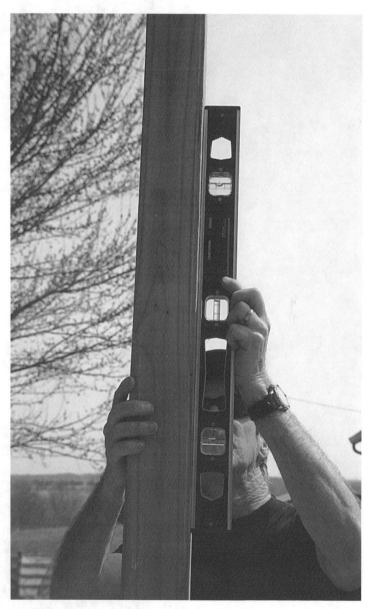

The top can be any number of materials, including translucent sheeting or solid roofing materials. Clear or translucent, as well as colored fiberglass panels, are available for roofing. These offer weather protection and shade, the amount of shade varying depending on the amount of light transference. Although a number of products are available, Filon Supalite is a clear, lightweight rooflight with a 3-inch pitch profile. Make sure when using these types of products to follow the manufacturer's pitch recommendations. Filon Supalite GRP rooflights are very tough and impact resistant, withstanding high winds and heavy hailstorms. It has exceptional durability and does not shatter over time, nor expand or shrink. It is easy to handle, pliable, and easy to cut with no special equipment. The porch shown utilized solid roofing materials and the underside was covered with white vinyl soffit material to match the white vinyl siding. In addition, a ceiling fan with light

It is extremely important that framing be constructed square and plumb.

A bevel gauge is used to lay out rafter angles.

was added. When installing ceiling fan/lights in screened-in porches, make sure to choose a unit that is approved for outdoor, wet, or damp use.

SCREENING

The next step is to add the screening. Screening is available in a range of materials including rustproof bronze, copper, or aluminum, as well as anodized aluminum with a baked-on finish and vinyl. Vinyl has become increasingly popular because it's easy to

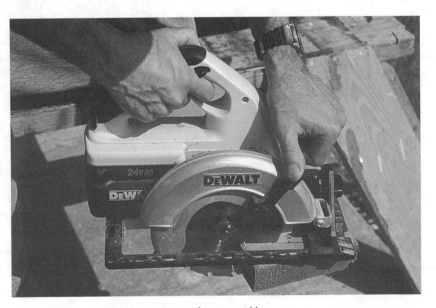

A cordless circular saw makes it easy to cut framing quickly.

work with and durable, although not as durable as some of the metal screens. The traditional method of installing screening on porches is to fasten the screen in place and cover the edges with batten boards. The porch shown was first painted, the screen applied, and then the painted batten boards nailed over the installed screen. The hardest chore is installing the screening without having sags or wrinkles. Cut the wire to fit the opening, overlapping by 1 inch. Fasten the top edge in place with staples. Pull the screening down and starting in the middle of the bottom edge, work toward each side, making sure the screening is smooth and not wrinkled. Then begin in the middle of each

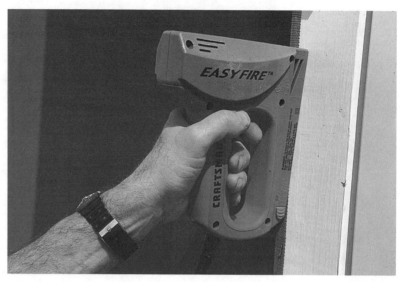

With framing complete, the porch is stained and finished or painted. Screening is then stapled in place and battens applied over the edges.

side and work to the outside edges again smoothing and stapling. Once the screening is fastened, nail the 1-×-2 (¾-×-1½-inch) batten boards over the screen edges.

FINISHING

Purchased wooden or prepainted metal or wood screen doors may be installed in the door openings, hinging the screen doors to batten boards and overlapping the posts and

A prepainted metal screen door is installed in place.

upper framing. Screen-door closures or springs and hooks can be used to hold the door or doors shut. Splashboards were installed along the bottom of the porch shown to prevent rainwater and mud from splashing up into the porch. The splashboards were cut from wood siding and fastened to the bottom blocking and posts after the screening was installed.

CHAPTER 2

PICNIC SHELTER

A PICNIC SHELTER CAN PROVIDE a place for enjoying a picnic, cooking on the barbeque grill, and other fun family activities, even in inclement weather. And, a picnic shelter can also provide shade from the summer sun for these activities. A provision can also be provided for hanging a porch swing. The shelter shown was constructed of native, rough-sawn red cedar, one of the most durable species for outdoor use. The support poles are actually 8-inch cedar logs with the bark removed and the logs "polished" with a wire brush. This is a very popular "Ozark" construction style and lends itself to a rustic backyard décor. Treated 6-×-6 wood posts can be substituted for the logs.

The first step is to lay out the location of the poles. Make sure they are laid out square. Temporarily drive stakes at the locations of the poles and then measure diagonally between the stakes. The measurements must be the same for a square construction. If they are not, shift the stakes as needed. Dig the holes for the poles and set them in place. Make sure they are plumb. This is rather difficult with the irregular shape of the logs. It is, however, important that their tops align in order to hold the support beams. The use of the support beams down on the log tops is also a means of constructing with the irregular sides poles. Once the poles are in the correct position and as plumb as you can get them, pour concrete around them in the holes. Once the concrete has set, cut the tops of the poles/posts off level using a chainsaw. Begin with the "lowest" pole and mark the height desired on it. Then use a string and string level to mark the tops of the other poles to be cut.

Picnic shelter shown is made of cedar log supports and rough-sawn cedar. It has a place for a picnic table, barbecue grill, and even has a porch swing support.

The picnic shelter roof is supported with a "post-and-beam" style construction. Cut the side beams to length and then cut the end beams to length. Cut the notches for the end beams to fit down over the side beams. Fit the side beams down over the pole tops and then fit the end beams down over the side beams. Make sure the beam construction is square. Use lag screws driven down through the beam ends and into the pole tops to anchor the beams in place. Then install a bolt up from the bottom of the ends of the side beams and into the top beams. The top lag bolts and nuts on the fastening bolts should be countersunk flush with the tops of the beams.

Cut the 2-×-6 rafters to the correct shape and length. Cut the notches in the rafters to fit down over the support beams. Cut the ridge plate to length and install the rafters, nailing their ends into the ridge plate and toenailing them down through their bottom edges into the support beams. Cut the collar ties to length and to the correct angles and nail them in place on the rafters. Then cut the ceiling "joists" to the correct length and fasten to the sides of the rafters. Note the one ceiling joist is actually a 4-×-4 beam sitting over the end beams. This provides a secure hanger for a porch swing. The ends should also have blocking from the beams to the underside of the rafters to provide a nailing surface for the end siding pieces.

Cut the roof sheathing to size and nail on the rafters. Note the roof sheathing extends one foot past the ends of the end beams. Nail the hanging rafters to the outside

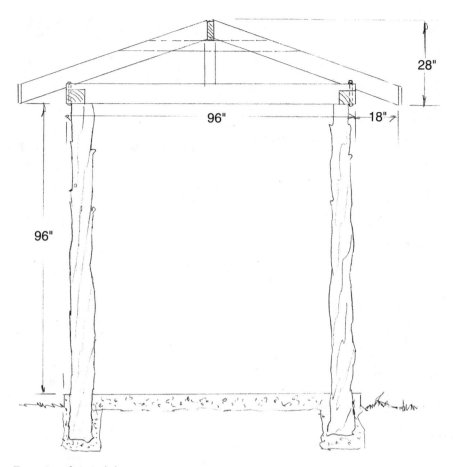

Front view of picnic shelter.

edges of the sheathing and then nail the 1-×-6 fascia to the hanging rafters and the ends of the support rafters. Add the drip edge if desired and shingle using composite shingles. Wooden shingles would also look nice on this building.

The underside of the ceiling joists, as well as the soffit, is finished off with cedar strips. This eliminates places for birds to roost under the roof.

The floor is formed and the concrete poured. Note the concrete extends out past the support poles.

Materials List

support poles: 8 in. × 10 ft., 4 req'd (or 6-×-6 treated posts)
side beams: 4 × 6 in. × 12 ft., 2 req'd
end beams: 4 × 6 in. × 8 ft., 2 req'd
rafters: 2 × 6 in. × 6 ft. (cut to fit), 9 pair req'd

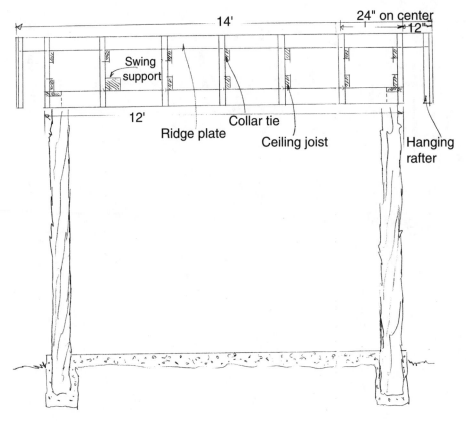

Side view of picnic shelter.

ridge plate: 2 × 6 in. × 14 ft., 1 req'd

collar ties: 1 × 4 in. × 6 ft., 7 req'd

ceiling joists: 2 × 4 in. × 8 ft., 6 req'd

swing support: 4 × 4 in. × 8 ft., 1 req'd

sheathing: ½ × 4 in. × 8 ft., 6 req'd

shingles: 2 square ft. req'd

ceiling: 96 square ft, req'd

fascia: 1 × 6 in. × 12 ft., 52 lineal feet req'd

soffit material: 18 in. × 28 lineal feet req'd

soffit material: 12 in. × 24 lineal feet req'd

CHAPTER 3

ATTACHED CARPORT

A CARPORT ATTACHED TO an existing building such as a garage, barn, shed, or the side of your house can provide economical shelter for vehicles, garden tractors, or other equipment. An attached carport is also fairly easy to construct. The carport shown utilizes basic and simple pole-building construction techniques. It may, however, not be strong enough or have enough roof slope for some high-snow areas. Again, check with local building codes and regulations.

The first step is to install the support header on the existing building. Mark the location of one end of the header. Then mark the other location. Make sure the header is level. Fasten the header in place with lag screws through the siding and into the studs of the existing building. Drop a plumb line from each corner of the header and mark this location on the bottom of the existing building. Then lay out the locations of the support posts. Beginning at one plumb line mark, attach a string to the building. Measure the length needed for one end, drive a stake, and fasten the string in place. Beginning at the second plumb line mark, measure for the opposite end, temporarily drive a stake, and add a second string line. Measure the distance between the two plumb-line marks for the length of the carport. Measure between the two stakes and adjust the stakes as needed to achieve the same distance.

Make sure the carport is laid out square with the existing building. One method of assuring square is with right-angle string lines. Beginning at one of the plumb-line marks, measure 3 feet out from the building on the string and mark this with a felt-tip pen. Measure 4 feet along the building wall and mark this measurement as well.

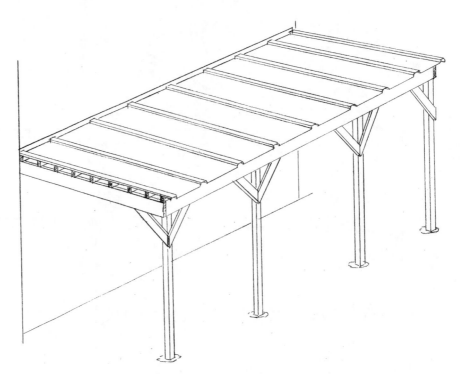

Attached carport is fairly simple to build yet provide shelter for vehicles of all kinds from cars and trucks to garden implements or ATVs.

Measure diagonally between the two marks. The measurement must be 5 feet to create a square corner. Move the string line end stake in or out to achieve the correct measurement. This creates a square corner for one end of the carport and determines the location of the corner post. Repeat for the opposite end and corner post. Then again, measure between the two stakes to make sure the length is correct. You can also check for squareness by measuring diagonally from the plumb line marks to the opposite outside corner locations. The measurements should be the same. With the corner post locations determined, run a string line from corner post to corner post and mark the locations of the other two posts.

The posts can be set on and anchored to concrete piers poured in holes in the ground. Or you may be able to utilize pre-cast piers. Another method is to set the posts in the concrete. In this case pressure-treated posts must be used. Again, check with local building authorities as to methods suitable for your area. When erecting the posts, make sure they are positioned correctly to create a square construction, again checking with a string and the triangular method. Make sure the posts are plumb, bracing them in place two ways with temporary stakes, and 2-×-4 braces.

Fasten the front support beam in place to the posts. This beam is actually made up of three 12-foot lengths. Then fasten the end beams to the posts overlapping the ends of the header and the front beam. Cut the angled braces and fasten to the post sides and

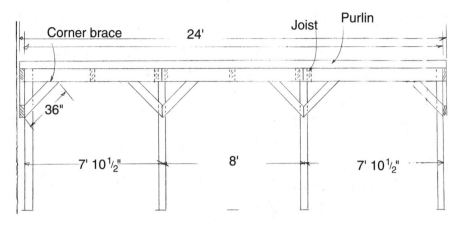

Carport front view.

toenail into the beams. Metal fastening plates can also be added inside these joints for more strength. The front braces have a 45-degree angle on both ends. The end braces are best cut by first cutting the bottom 45-degree angle, positioning a brace in place and marking the top angle to fit the end beam. Fasten the rafters between the header and front beam using joist hangers, and nailing in from the front beam. Fasten the purlins down over the rafters. These can be toenailed or utilize metal support plates.

Install metal, fiberglass, or polycarbonate panels such as SunTuf over the purlins. Add the flashing as needed at the back edge. You may also wish to add gravel or even pour a concrete floor.

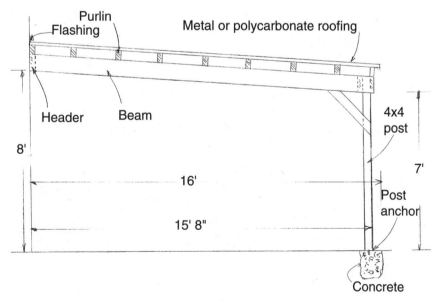

Carport side view.

Materials List

support posts: 4 × 4 in. × 10 ft., 4 req'd

headers: 2 × 8 in. × 12 ft., 2 req'd

joists: 2 × 6 in. × 16 ft., 6 req'd

front beams: 2 × 8 in. × 8 ft., 3 req'd

end beams: 2 × 8 in. × 16 ft., 2 req'd

braces: 2 × 6 in. × 3 ft., 8 req'd

purlins: 2 × 4 in. × 12 ft., 18 req'd

roofing of choice: 16 × 24 ft.

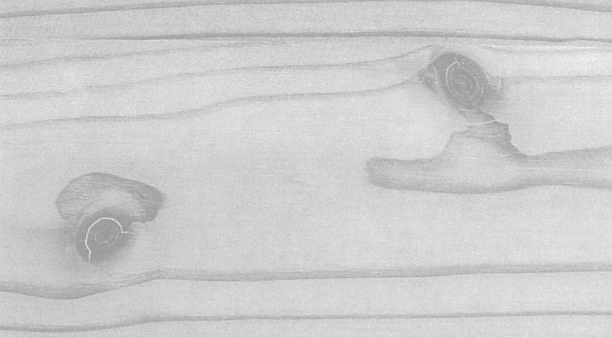

BACKYARD STRUCTURES

A "mini" pole shed, garden tool shed, greenhouse, and garage workshop are complicated projects, but well within the reach of the average do-it-yourselfer—if done in steps. These projects can not only provide valuable storage space, but also increase the value of your property.

CHAPTER 1

DRIVE-THRU "MINI" POLE SHED

TIRED OF MOVING THE riding mower every time I wanted to get to the tiller and vice-versa, I designed this garden shed with doors on each end. This two-door design allows me easy access to all my garden tools—whether they're stored in the back or the front. I can even pull a garden tractor with implement or trailer behind it, driving in one door, and then when I want to use the tractor again, I simply open the opposite door and drive out.

Before I could build my shed, however, a problem had to be solved. The only location for the shed was on a slope where I could have constructed a wooden-floored shed or used a concrete pad. In both cases, this would have added to the cost, and I wanted an economical, easy-to-drive-into shed. The result is a "mini" pole-barn. Pole construction is one of the most economical methods of building construction, and it's also relatively easy. The small pole shed shown is also an excellent "practice" project for anyone wishing to construct a large pole building. The basic construction techniques shown can also be used to construct a larger garden building.

Basic construction consists of setting poles in holes in the ground and anchoring the poles in place with concrete. Pole barns are often made of round poles, but square posts

A garden shed with doors on each end provides easy, drive-through storage for garden equipment. You can also park a tiller at one end and a mower at the other. Pole-style building is also an economical approach to a sloping lot.

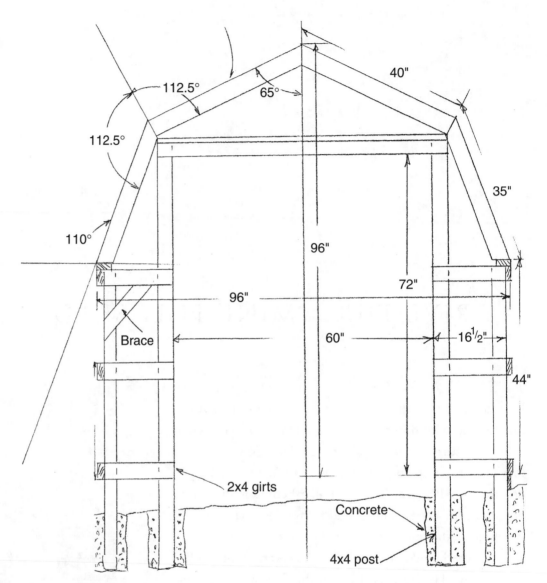

Shed end view.

can also be used, as in the shed shown. The poles or posts must be pressure treated or otherwise suitable for in-ground use. After the posts are set, girts, or horizontal nailing boards, are nailed to the posts and siding is anchored to the girts. Typically, a truss roof is then used to construct an open-type building.

Before you begin construction, contact your local building authorities regarding any rules and regulations for pole buildings, as well as the recommended depth for the holes containing the poles. Also check for any standard rules, regulations, and permits needed for constructing any building. The shed shown is permanent, not movable, so it may be subject to additional permits and regulations.

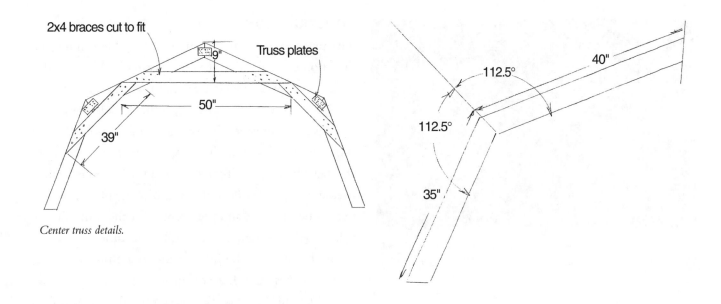

2x4 braces cut to fit

Truss plates

9"

50"

39"

112.5°

112.5°

40"

35"

Center truss details.

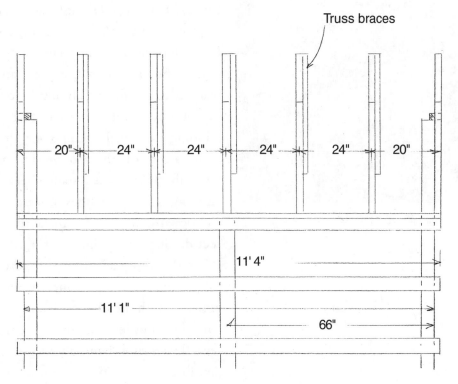

Truss braces

20"   24"   24"   24"   24"   20"

11' 4"

11' 1"

66"

Shed side view.

The first step is to lay out the building. Use short stakes to locate the poles. Measure diagonally between the corner stakes to establish a square building.

Dig the holes to the depth needed for your particular soil and region.

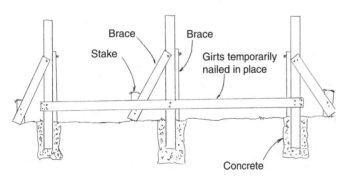

Posts are located in the proper position, plumbed, and braced. A temporary "girt" board helps establish location. Then pour concrete around the posts.

CONSTRUCTION

The first step is to lay out the building. Determine the direction of it, aligning it with existing buildings as desired. Drive small stakes at each of the four corner locations as per the wall lengths, with the outside corners of the stakes the outside measurements of the poles. (Note: this is not the final building size, because the 2-×-4 horizontals must also be figured in the final measurement.) Measure diagonally from the outside edge of a stake corner to the opposite and then repeat for the other diagonal. These measurements should be the same to ensure a square building. If the measurements are not the same, shift the stakes until they are equal.

Dig the holes to the recommended depth. This may vary, but 2 feet would be considered adequate for this size building, in most locations. Position the poles in place in the holes. On sloping lots, make sure the lower slope poles are not set so deep their tops are not high enough. Plumb the posts and brace them in place. Measure diagonally, inside to inside of the corner posts, and relocate them to reestablish a square building. Tack-nail a temporary girt to the posts and about a foot off the ground. This not only helps to maintain the correct distance between the posts, but also aligns the post sides. Locate the doorposts and additional side posts and make sure they are the correct distance from the other posts as well as plumb. Brace them in place. Once all posts are properly located and braced, mix concrete and pour around the posts. Smooth the top of the concrete flush or slightly above ground level. Allow the concrete to cure for several days, and then remove the braces and temporary girts.

If on a sloping lot, position the lowest to ground level, bottom-side girt in place. Make sure it is level. Install the end girts, positioning them flush with the ends of the side girts and then positioning them level.

Fasten the lower girts in place, making sure they are level. Measure up for the side posts and mark their heights, making sure these are level all around the building. Then mark around the posts and cut them off at the correct height.

(Note: the girts are installed in place and the siding added, then the door openings cut out.) Finally, install the next lower-side girt. Once the bottom girts are in place, install the "skirting" boards of treated materials. On a sloping lot this may entail cutting some bottom edges of the skirting boards at an angle. Leave off the end skirt board until the siding is installed and doors are cut out.

Measure up from the bottom girts and mark the locations of the top side girts on each end post and the center-side posts. Make sure the girts are level. A string level and line can be used for establishing these final pole heights or you can use a girt, held in place and leveled, to mark the locations. Square around the posts and cut them to the correct height. Fasten the top-side girts in place. These will protrude 1½ inches past each post end. Then position a top-side plate flush with the outside edges of the top girt and fasten it down on the top-side girts and to the tops of the posts. Add the middle girts. Fasten a girt to the end starting at the top-side girt and to the opposite corner post. Make sure it is level. Repeat for the opposite end. Then locate and position the middle-end girts. Finally, position and anchor the opposite top-side girt and the middle girt.

Measure the height needed for the over-the-door girt on the doorposts. Make sure this is level and then cut each doorpost off to the correct height. Fasten the girt in place, then again nail a top plate down on each and flush with the outside edge of the

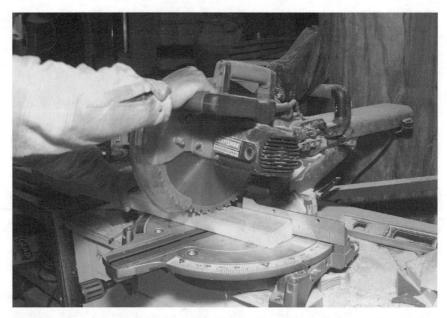

The roof is constructed of trusses. A miter saw easily cuts the angles precisely.

girt. Repeat for the opposite end. Pole barns are typically braced with 45-degree angle braces anchored to each post and toenailed or screwed to the underside of the top girts. This creates the "wind-bracing" needed.

The next step is to build the trusses for the roof. Although construction is fairly simple, properly laying out the trusses and making the cuts at the proper angles is extremely important. Make a "try-fit" truss to help ensure you get them right. Cut each piece to the correct size and angle. A radial arm or miter saw is excellent for this because the angles can be set precisely or you can use a bevel square set to the proper angles and make the cuts with a portable circular saw. Lay the pieces on a flat, smooth surface and fasten together with metal truss plates or hardboard plywood braces. Make sure the outside bottom corners are at 8 feet. Do not add the 2-×-4 braces at this time. Try-fit the sample truss on both ends as well as in the middle of the building. (You'll need a helper for this chore.) Adjust any angles or lengths as needed. Once you're satisfied with the fit, lay the sample truss on a smooth, flat surface. To speed up the process and provide more accurate truss construction, set up the saw and make all same-angle

Make a master truss and try-fit in place. Then build the remaining trusses by laying the pieces of another truss on top of the master truss and using it as a "pattern."

The basic building framing completed. Note the end girts are installed over the door openings and the openings cut out later.

cuts. Then set up for the next angle and make all those cuts. Once all pieces are cut, position them down on the "master" truss and fasten together with truss plates on both sides, as well as with the 2-×-4 braces. Note the two end trusses do not have the 2-×-4 braces.

With a helper, erect one end truss. Toenail it to the top plate. Use a 2-×-4 end brace temporarily nailed to the end girts and to the top corner of the truss, to hold the truss in place. Short blocks are nailed down on the topside plates and the trusses nailed into these blocks for additional strength. Position two more trusses in place, making sure they are located in the proper position. Then tack-nail a temporary 2-×-4 brace across their tops, again making sure that they are positioned properly. Repeat for the opposite side. Then erect and install the remaining trusses, anchoring the end truss again with a temporary 2-×-4 brace to the end girts.

Now you're ready to install the siding. Position the end siding panels in place and anchor them solidly. Locate the corners of the door openings and the roof truss angles by boring small holes through the siding at the proper locations from the inside. Use a

Siding is installed.

The angled cuts and door openings are marked from the inside using a small drill bit. A straightedge is used between the holes on the outside to mark the cuts.

Then the cuts are made with a portable circular saw.

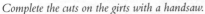
Complete the cuts on the girts with a handsaw.   *Sheathing is installed on the roof and the roof shingled.*

straightedge to mark between the holes. A portable circular saw, saber saw, or even a reciprocating saw can then be used to cut off the excess plywood at the top ends and to
make the door cutouts. Once the door openings have been made, use 2-×-4 blocking
flush with the outside edges of the posts, between the girts and between the posts and
the siding. Cut the siding for the sides and install it one half inch lower than the top
edge of the top-side plates.

    Install the roof sheathing on the lower roof sides, allowing it to protrude 4 inches
over each end. Then cut and install the upper roof sheathings in place. Cut the end
"hanging" rafters to the proper shape and size and fasten them to the protruding
sheathing. Apply roofing felt and nail the asphalt shingles in place on the roof. Cut the
trim to width and fasten on the corners, at the roof edge and around the doors. Then
add the "soffit."

Finish details include adding the trim ripped from 1 x 12s.

The doors are constructed from the cutout siding pieces.

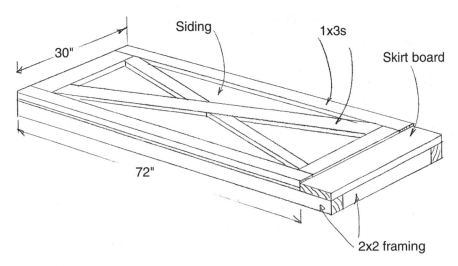

Door detail.

The final construction step is to assemble the doors and hang them in place. The doors are constructed using the siding cutouts from the ends. For strength, use 2-×-2 backing and add 1-×-3 trim boards to the door fronts. The building can now be painted in traditional "barn red" and white trim, or painted or stained any color pattern desired to match or complement existing buildings.

Materials List

treated posts: 4 × 4 in. × 8 ft., 6 req'd

treated posts: 4 × 4 in. × 10 ft., 2 req'd

2 × 4s × 12 ft., 8 req'd

2 × 4s × 8 ft., 30 req'd

wood siding: 4 × 8 ft., 7 req'd

sheathing: ½ in. 4 × 8 ft., 6 req'd

1 × 6s × 8 ft. 20 treated, req'd (for building with
  ground slope shown)

#60 bags concrete mix: 10 req'd

truss plates: 4 × 6 in., 36 req'd

sheathing clips: 18 req'd

#15 felt: 1 roll

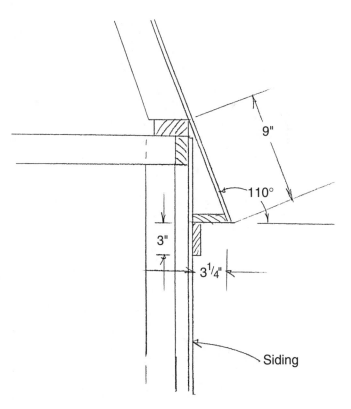

Soffit detail.

asphalt or composite shingles: 2 squares, or 6 bundles

roof drip edge: 5 req'd

roofing nails: 3 lbs. req'd

#16 common nails: 3 lbs. req'd

#4 galvanized nails: 3 lbs. req'd

butt hinges and screws: 4 in., 8 req'd

padlock hasp: 2 req'd

CHAPTER 2

GARDEN TOOL SHED

THE AGE-OLD "SHTICK" about a rake handle smacking you in the face when you step on the teeth isn't funny. It's happened to me—more than once. Properly storing rakes, hoes, shovels, and other long-handled tools is often a problem. They can be hung up in a garage or garden shed, but usually end up right at the door, where they fall down, and present a danger. The garden tool shed shown solves the challenge of long-handled tool storage and at the same time provides a separate storage area attached to a garage or garden shed with tools at hand. This shed could also hold trashcans. The shed shown doesn't have a back, but a back could be installed to make the shed free-standing if desired. The shed shown would, however, be susceptible to toppling over very easily, so should be "staked" or fastened in place in some manner.

The siding of the shed shown is hardboard (barn siding) and requires two 4-×-8-foot sheets. First, crosscut 24 inches off the end of one 4-×-8-foot sheet. This creates the top. Rip the 6-foot piece to the correct width for the sides, and then cut their angled ends. Some of the framing is constructed of 2-×-2 (1½-×-1½ inches) materials. The first step is to rip the 2 × 2s from 2 × 4s. Cut the front and back support 2 × 2s to length. Fasten a side down over these framing members. Next, measure and cut the bottom and topside pieces to length, making sure the angles are correct on the top pieces. Note the bottom pieces are 2 × 4s. Fasten these between the upright members. All siding should be fastened in place with non-corrosive fasteners. An air brad nailer works great for this step. Repeat for the opposite side.

A handy, attached garden tool shed takes the hassle and danger out of storing long-handled garden tools inside your garage.

Stand the sides upright and cut the upper and lower back 2-× -4 cross members to the correct length. Position the cross pieces between the sides and fasten the sides to them with non-corrosive "decking" screws. Cut and fasten the front 2-×-4 cross members in place in the same manner. Stand the unit upright. Cut and install the floor joists between the front and back lower cross members and then cut and install a ¾-inch floor over the floor joists, notching to fit around the 2-×-2 uprights.

Cut the 2-×-2 doorframe members and fit them in place between the front crosspieces. The tops are held in place with a block over the back of the top crosspiece and door upright. The bottoms are anchored to a spacer block positioned between it and the side upright.

Use a carpenter's square to make sure the assembly is square. Then rip the front siding pieces and install them in place. Rip the upper and lower siding cross pieces and install them in place.

Rip the 1½-inch trim pieces from a treated 1 × 6. Cut the front uprights to length, making sure their tops follow the angle of the sides. Fasten in place with No. 8d non-corrosive nails. An air nailer, such as the Craftsman utility coil nailer, is perfect for this chore. Cut the upper, lower, and back-side trim boards and install them in place. Then cut the front top and bottom trim pieces and install them as well.

Cut the door siding piece to size. Then cut the inside uprights from 2 × 2s to the correct length and fasten the siding piece down over the uprights. Cut the bottom and

A portable circular saw makes it quick and easy to cut 2 x 4s to length.

An air brad stapler makes it a cinch to attach siding.

top cross 2-×-2 pieces and fasten them in place. The door also has 1½-inch trim on the outside. Cut the side door trim pieces to the correct length and fasten in place down over the siding with No. 8d non-corrosive nails. Fasten the upper and lower cross pieces between them. Angled door cross trim pieces add to the décor. Cut these to fit and fasten in place. Then hang the door and install the hook. Add a latch, or hasp, if you prefer to have a means of locking the shed.

Cut the interior rafters to size, following the angles of the front and back cross members. One method of doing this is to lay a rafter across the top of the cross members and then use a block of wood held against both pieces to mark the angle on the rafters. Install between the cross members. Install the hardboard top piece for the roof down over the rafters. The top can be left as is, but it's best to apply roll roofing or composite shingles to match an existing building. Paint or stain to match existing buildings.

Anchor the completed shed to the outside of a building with screws through the top back cross piece into the building. Apply caulking on the back of the roof edge and to the adjoining building. Finally, fasten the top back trim strip down over the caulk and to the shed top and the adjoining building.

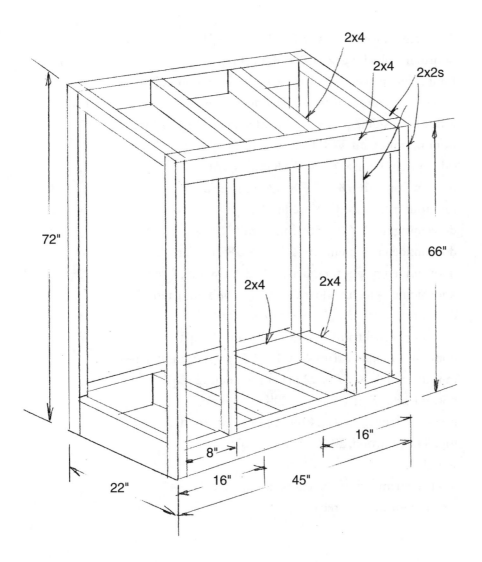

Materials List

sides: ⅜-in. siding, 22 × 72 in., cut to angle, 2 req'd

side front upright: 2 × 2 × 66 in., 2 req'd

side rear upright: 2 × 2 × 72 in., 2 req'd

side bottom cross member: 2 × 4 × 19 in., 2 req'd

side top cross member: 2 × 2 × 19 in., 2 req'd

rear bottom back and front cross members: 2 × 4 × 42 in., 2 req'd

front top and rear cross members: 2 × 4 × 42 in., 2 req'd

floor joists: 2 × 4 × 19 in., 2 req'd

rafters: 2 × 4 × 19 in., 2 req'd

floor: ¾-plywood × 22 × 45 in., cut to fit, 1 req'd

doorframe uprights: 2 × 2 × 59 in., 2 req'd

doorframe blocking: 2 × 2 × 8 in., 4 req'd

front siding pieces: ⅜-in. hardboard × 16 × 66 in., 2 req'd

upper front siding piece: ⅜-in. hardboard × 3¼ × 29 in., 1 req'd

lower front siding piece: ⅜-in. hardboard × 3½ × 29 in., 1 req'd

front upright trim: ¾ × 1½ × 59 in., 2 req'd

side upright trim: ¾ × 1½ × 66 in., 2 req'd

bottom front trim: ¾ × 3½ × 42 in., 1 req'd

top front trim: ¾ × 3¼ × 42 in., 1 req'd

door uprights: 2 × 2 x 58½ in., 2 req'd

door inside cross members: 2 × 2 × 28½ in., 2 req'd

door inside upright members: 2 × 2 × 58½ in., 2 req'd

door siding: ⅜ in. hardboard × 28 ½ × 58½ in., 1 req'd

door upright trim: ¾ × 1½ × 58½ in., 2 req'd

door horizontal trim: ¾ × 1½ × 28½ in., 2 req'd

door cross member trim: ¾ × 1½ × 62 in., cut to fit, 2 req'd

topside trim: ¾ × 1½ × 22 in., cut to angle, 2 req'd

bottom-side trim: ¾ × 1½ × 20½ in., 2 req'd

back-side trim: ¾ × 1½ × 69 in., angle cut to fit, 2 req'd

top: ⅜ in. plywood, 22 × 45 in., 1 req'd

shingles to fit

top back trim strip: ¾ × 1½ × 45 in., 1 req'd

screen door hook: 1 req'd

CHAPTER 3

GREENHOUSE

A SMALL GREENHOUSE CAN BE invaluable to the serious gardener. The greenhouse shown is covered with Suntuf polycarbonate panels. Suntuf panels keep out the sun's harmful UV rays, yet promote healthy plant growth. The plans of the greenhouse shown are courtesy of Suntuf.

The first step is to level the ground and build a foundation. A concrete pad is ideal for supporting the house. Make sure, however, you check local building codes for pad and/or footing and foundation construction requirements in your area. Actually, gravel can be used for the floor, but the walls should be supported and anchored by a footing. An alternative would be to build the house on 2-×-6 skids. The greenhouse then becomes a "portable" building that can be moved where desired.

Until you're ready to install, retain the Suntuf corrugated polycarbonate panels in their original package. Ideally, the panels should be stored on a flat pallet in a dry, shaded place and avoid extreme humidity, dust, or direct sunlight. During installation, do not stand or walk on the corrugated panels that lack adequate support. Verify that the UV-protected sides of the installed sheets are facing out to the sun.

Due to the moisture conditions of a greenhouse, the framing consists of all pressure-treated wood, such as Wolmanized Natural Select Wood. Lay out the framing for the front wall on a flat, smooth surface. Erect the front wall and brace it in place. Make sure the wall is square and plumb. Then construct and erect the two side walls, and finally the rear wall. Make sure all walls are plumb and square. Then connect the walls with 2-×-4 wall girts at the corners. Angle braces must be installed at each corner of the

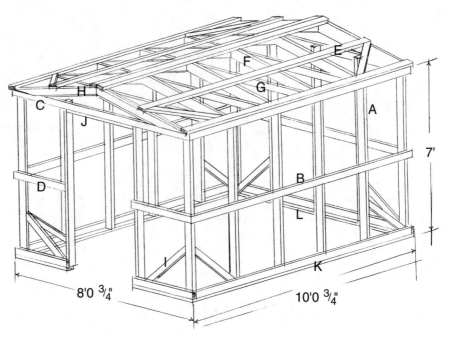

Greenhouse.

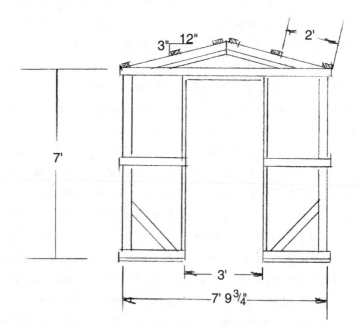

Front view.

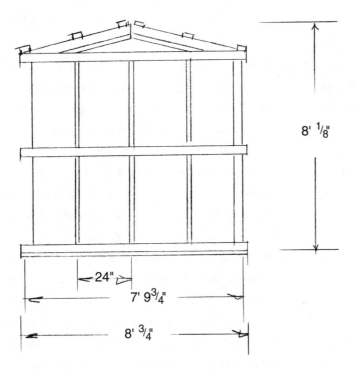

8' 1/8"

24"

7' 9 3/4"

8' 3/4"

Back view.

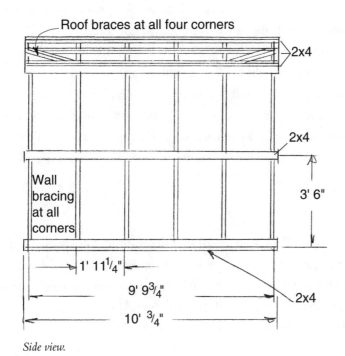

Roof braces at all four corners

2x4

2x4

3' 6"

Wall bracing at all corners

1' 11 1/4"

9' 9 3/4"

10' 3/4"

2x4

Side view.

building and the end walls. The base of the building must be anchored in accordance to local building codes.

Fasten the ceiling joists in place and then add the rafters and purlins. Joist hangers and metal rafter plates make it easy to install and join these members. Install the front and rear rafter blocking that is needed to provide the nailing surface for the wall panels to fasten to the gable. Finally, add the bracing on the lower corners of the roof. Make sure the building is constructed square and solidly connected.

For best results in some geographic areas, ventilation may be required. This can be automatic opening greenhouse windows and even a fan if needed. If a painted or stained frame is needed, complete the painting before installing Suntuf corrugated polycarbonate panels.

The next step is to install the Suntuf panels. They are installed using special Suntuf fasteners through predrilled holes. To drill, back up the sheet with scrap wood. Use a sharp steel drill bit, a slow speed, and a moderate amount of muscle. Too much pressure will cause the hole to chip out unevenly. Too much speed will draw the sheet up onto the threads of the drill bit. Draw fasteners down only enough to secure the panels. Overtightening can warp the paneling and create leakage problems.

For making straight cuts in sheets of more than 3mm thickness, use a circular saw or band saw. A medium-to-fine toothed blade (6 to 12 teeth per inch) works best. Use a cutting speed of 300 to 400 feet per minute. For thinner sheets, careful cutting with a band saw is possible, but shears or a router allows for greater precision. Hold the sheet down when cutting. Work the saw firmly, but do not force it.

Use the special floor and wood closure to seal off the panel corrugations. Once the roof has been installed, add the Suntuf ridge cap.

Note: building code requirements are not taken into consideration in the design of this structure. Nor are unique snow and wind load conditions, which are present in some areas. These details should be used only as a reference. Consult your municipality or township for local building code requirements before beginning construction.

Materials List

A. wall studs: 2 × 4 in. × 7 ft., 17 req'd
B. side wall girts: 2 × 4 in. × 10 ft. ¾ in., miter cut corners, 6 req'd
C. end wall girts: 2 × 4 in. × 8 ft. ¾ in., miter cut corners, 4 req'd
D. front wall girts: 2 × 4 in. × 2 ft. 6 in., miter cut corners, 4 req'd
E. roof purlins: 2 × 4 in. × 10 ft. ¾ in., 6 req'd
F. rafters: 2 × 6 in. × 4 ft. 1⅞ in., notched, 12 req'd
G. ceiling joists: 2 × 4 in. × 8 ft. ¾ in., 6 req'd

H. blocking: 2 × 4 in. × 4 ft., 4 req'd

I. corner angle braces: 2 × 4 in. × 2 ft. 6 in., 12 req'd

J. top doorjamb: 2 × 4 in. × 3 ft., 1 req'd

K. base of structure, pressure-treated lumber: 2 × 4 in. × 10 ft. ¾ in., 2 req'd

L. base of structure, pressure-treated lumber: 2 × 4 in. × 8 ft. ¾ in., 2 req'd

M. screen/storm door: 3 × 6 ft. 8 in., 1 req'd

N. Suntuf clear corrugated panels: 26 in. × 8 ft., 16 req'd

O. Suntuf clear corrugated panels: 26 in. × 12 ft., 5 req'd

P. Suntuf clear ridge cap: 4 ft. 2 in. req'd

Q. WoodTite fasteners: 2 in., 7 boxes req'd

R. foam closures: 36 in., 16 bags req'd

S. universal wood closures: 6 ft., 8 req'd

T. nails, 16d: 9 lbs. req'd

U. paint: 1 gallon req'd

CHAPTER 4

TWO-CAR GARAGE/WORKSHOP

ONE OF THE MOST "imposing" projects to build in this book is a two-car garage/workshop. The building was actually designed by the author as a workshop, but also doubles as vehicle storage when needed. Construction is standard house-framing style except for the purchased trusses. Pre-engineered trusses make building quicker

and easier for a first-timer, but they do require help in erecting. The building is designed to sit on a standard concrete slab floor and this can consist of either frost or no-frost construction. Check with local building authorities on code rules and regulations regarding slab construction in your area.

LAYOUT

The building and slab is first laid out with batter boards and string lines. To make sure the building is laid out square, use the triangle method to initially create the first right angle corner. Position one string line and then temporarily position the adjoining string line. Measure 8 feet on the first string line and

A 24-x-32 foot building makes a dandy shop, two-car garage, or both. The building shown is fairly straightforward and utilizes purchased trusses and no rake overhang for easy building.

The building is held in place with J-bolts inserted in the concrete. After the concrete has set, lay a bottom plate next to the bolts and mark the bolt holes.

make a mark. Measure 6 feet on the temporary line and mark that location. Then measure between the two marks on the strings. The distance should be 10 feet. Shift the temporary string in or out to achieve that measurement. Then measure and set the next two lines to create the building outline. Measure diagonally between the two corner stakes, and then measure diagonally between the opposite two stakes—the distances should be the same. If not, shift the stakes until the measurements are the same. Pour the foundation and floor as per local code rules. Make sure anchor bolts are installed as per code rules. For more information on pouring the floor, see Section II, Chapter 1, Working with Concrete.

BUILDING WALLS

The walls of the 24-×-32-foot building are each laid out in two sections for easy erecting. Before beginning framing make sure you have the proper rough-opening dimensions for any doors and windows. The building shown has two windows on one side, an entry door, window on one end, and two 9-foot garage doors on the front.

Begin with the back wall, or the wall with the entry door and one window. Lay a 12-foot bottom plate next to the anchor bolts inserted in the concrete and mark the bolt locations on the bottom plate board. Drill the holes in the bottom plate for the anchor bolts and try-fit the board to make sure the bottom plate properly fits down

Lay the top plate next to the bottom plate and lay out the walls, marking locations of all studs, window and door openings, etc.

The walls are constructed by laying the precut studs between the plates at their proper locations. Each wall is constructed in two sections.

The outer ends of both end walls have two studs with a spacer stud or blocks between them to create an inside corner that can be finished off.

over the anchor bolts. Then lay the 12-foot top plate next to the bottom plate. Using a carpenter's square and tape measure, measure and mark the locations of the studs on both the bottom and top plate. Note the outer end corner studs consist of two studs with blocking between. This provides the corner needed to finish off the inside of the building with materials such as sheetrock or paneling. Mark the locations of the window and door openings. These rough openings should be about 1½ inches larger all around than the finished door or window. This allows for casings and shims to install the window or door square. It's best to purchase windows and doors first and follow the rough opening sizes indicated by the manufacturer. Mark the locations of the jack studs to hold the door or window headers, as well as the cripple studs below and above the windows. Lay the marked plates on edge and fasten the precut studs between the plates using two No. 16d nails at each stud and on each end. Construct the headers. Doubled 2 × 6s with spacers to bring them to the width of the studs, with cripple studs above, can be used for openings of 36 inches or less. Or you may prefer to use doubled 2 × 10s to create solid headers as this eliminates cutting the short cripple studs above the window header. The jack studs are nailed in place to the bottom plate, and to the adjoining studs. Then the headers are fastened in place over the jack studs. Finally, cripple studs are installed as needed. Wind bracing should be used where possible, as long as it doesn't run through a window or door. These prevent the building walls from "racking" out of square. Make sure you follow local code rules on this step.

Door and window headers are formed by first nailing spacers between the 2-x-10 header boards.

Wind bracing can be metal strips, or 1 × 4s. The latter are "let-in" to the studs. First, make sure the wall section is square. Use a carpenter's square and also measure diagonally from corner to corner and shift the wall section to make sure it is square. Then place a 1 × 4 for the wind bracing on either the inside or outside of the studs, and diagonally 45 degrees from top to bottom plates. Temporarily tack nail the brace in

The header boards are then fastened together.

The headers are nailed in place on the top plate.

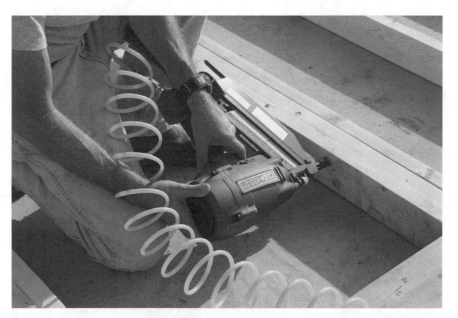

And the jack and cripple studs nailed to support the headers.

Wind bracing, in this case 1 x 4s let into the studs on the outside, provides support. The first step is to measure diagonally from corner to corner and make sure the wall section is square.

Tack nail wind bracing in place and mark each side where it crosses a stud or plate.

Use a portable circular saw with the blade set to cut just ¾-inch and cut notches in the 2 x 4s.

place, and mark the location of the bracing on each stud. Using a portable circular saw set to cut ¾ inch deep, make a cut at each mark on the stud, and then make several cuts between the marked cuts. Use a chisel and hammer to knock out the cut pieces. Fasten the wind bracing in place with No. 8d nails. Another type of bracing is called "block bracing." It is used when full 2-×-4 bracing is required. The blocks are cut diagonally and toenailed between the studs. Once the first section is completed, repeat these steps on the other end wall section.

Then use a chisel to remove the material between the notches.

Make sure the wall section is square again, then fasten the wind bracing in place.

Stand the first section in place, lifting it up and over the anchor bolts. Plumb the wall section using a 4-foot level and brace it well in place with 2 × 4s run to stakes driven in the ground outside the building. Stand the next section up with it's inside end butting against the first section. Make sure their edges meet properly at the bottom plates. Plumb and brace this section as well. Fasten the two sections together with 16d nails through the two joining studs. Make sure the entire wall is well braced

The two end wall sections are stood up and braced in place, anchoring them together at their center studs.

The bottom plates are anchored with washers and nuts over the J-bolts.

Once an end wall has been erected, a section of each side wall can be erected, plumbed, braced, and the corners fastened together.

Tie plates are nailed on top of the top plates, crossing the corners to tie them together. Space the tie plates so that their joints don't cross the top plate joints. This straightens the wall.

with 2 × 4s running out to stakes driven in the ground. Add the 2 × 4 tie plate over the tops of the top plate, using a 16-foot 2 × 4 for one tie plate. This creates a strong overlap of the wall joints. The tie plates should be inset 3½ inches at each end. This allows for the side wall tie-plates to lap over the end walls and join the corners together.

Construct the opposite end wall in the same manner. This wall also consists of two sections with a garage door in each section. The doubled 2-×-10 headers must be well supported with jack studs on each end. Stand each section up, plumb and brace it, then again add the tie plates to the top.

Then construct the two side walls, again in two sections. These walls are measured to fit between the two end walls. Erect and fasten them in place at all corners and in their centers. Then run the tie plates over the ends of the end walls and the tops of the side walls. Fasten all tie plates 24 inches on center with No. 16d nails.

ROOF

The roof framing consists of purchased 24-foot pre-engineered trusses. Before erecting the first end truss, ¾-inch blocking must be nailed to the outside of the first and last trusses in order to fasten siding in place. The trusses provide a quick means of roof framing, but you will need help in erecting them. Even trusses of this size are heavy and they can be dangerous if not handled properly. The trusses must first be

The end trusses must have 1-x-3 blocking to provide nailers for the siding.

lifted up onto the side walls, with their tops hanging down. Start at the back end of the building, lift one truss end up and place on the wall. Then lift the opposite end, making sure the first end doesn't slide off. At this point, the truss is hanging upside down in the building. I like to temporarily nail a block on the outer edge of each end wall and a support on the end that reaches high enough to prevent the truss from falling outward. This block prevents the first or end truss from sliding off the

The first end truss is erected, fastened in place, plumbed and well braced.

end when it is erected. A push-pole with a fork on the end created by fastening a short 2 × 4 to the end of a longer 2 × 4 can be used to push and swing the truss top up in position. It will take three persons to erect the truss. One swings and pushes the top up in place while the other two make sure the ends don't slide out of place. They then anchor the ends of the trusses in place to the wall plates. One method of doing this is with blocks fastened to the tie plates and the truss ends nailed into the block. Some localities may require hurricane-bracing plates. The first truss must also be plumbed and braced solidly in place with 2 × 4s running out to stakes driven in the ground. Erect the second truss in the same manner. Use temporary 2-×-4 braces across the two trusses at the top, making sure the second truss is plumb as well. Repeat until all trusses are erected. Once you reach an 8-foot span you can begin fastening sheathing in place to hold the trusses permanently in place. Begin the sheathing at the bottom edges of the trusses, working upward to the ridge. Make sure the sheathing is started square and that

Blocks are nailed on the tie plates as a nailer and locator for the truss ends.

Trusses are heavy and you'll need at least three people to erect them. The truss ends are positioned up on the walls with the toe hanging down.

A 2-x-4 push pole with a 2-x-4 fork on its end is used by the center worker to push the top of the truss up in position, while workers on the wall ends steady the truss ends in place.

The tops of the trusses are plumbed and temporarily anchored in place with 2 x 4s across their tops.

Truss hangers, or hurricane strips, and toenailing into the truss stop blocks is used to anchor the truss ends.

Rip 2-x-6 truss end supports to match the angle of the trusses and fasten in place. Then install the fascia.

Sheathing is applied over the trusses, removing the 2-x-4 braces and making sure the trusses are spaced properly on 24-inch centers their entire lengths.

the 8-foot joints meet in the center of the trusses. Shift the truss tops to align them properly and make sure the end of each sheet of sheathing meets over a truss and is nailed to a truss. Stagger the joints of the sheets on the trusses. The opposite end truss must also have blocking for siding.

FINISHING

The siding is then installed. Again, make sure the first sheet is installed plumb. The lower end of the siding should extend below the slab or foundation about one-half

Siding is installed.

The gable rake boards installed.

inch. Fasten the siding in place with No. 8d non-corrosive siding or casing nails. They should be spaced 6 inches on center at panel edges and 12 inches on center on the intermediate studs. Apply Z-flashing on the gable ends. Cut and install the siding up on the gable ends and down over the flashing. Apply the fascia and soffit materials as well as the 1-×-2 trim boards at corners and other areas as indicated.

And the roof shingled.

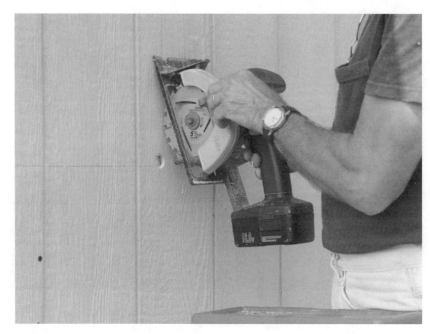

The openings for doors and windows are cut.

Doors and windows are installed.

Trim is painted and installed.

Apply the roofing felt and drip edge. Then follow the manufacturer's instructions on the shingle bundles to install the composite shingles. Extend the shingles one-half inch past the trim board faces.

Install the doors and windows following the manufacturer's instructions. Make sure the windows are resting on a doubled 2-×-4 sill plate. Then add the door and window trim. Paint as desired.

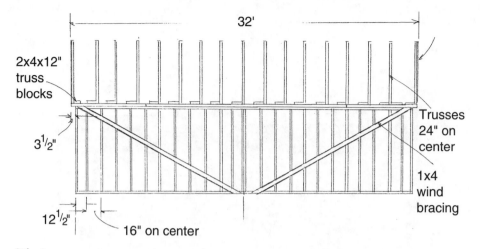

2x4x12"
truss
blocks

3½"

12½"

16" on center

Trusses
24" on
center

1x4
wind
bracing

Side view.

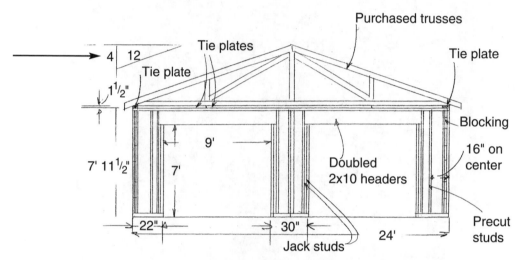

Purchased trusses

Tie plates

Tie plate

Tie plate

4 | 12

1½"

Blocking

7' 11½"

9'

7'

Doubled
2x10 headers

16" on
center

22"

30"

24'

Jack studs

Precut
studs

Front view.

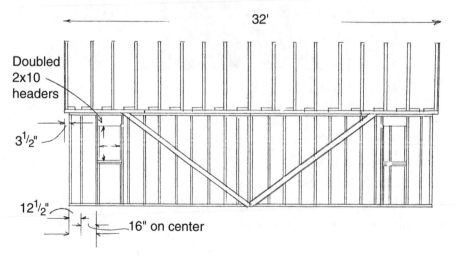

32'

Doubled
2x10
headers

3½"

12½"

16" on center

Side view.

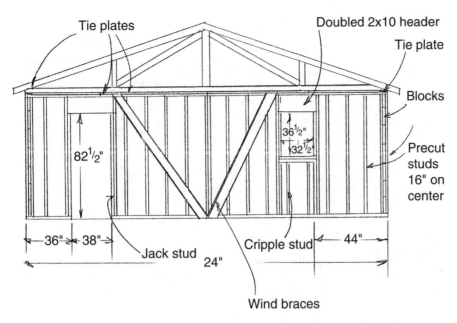

Back view.

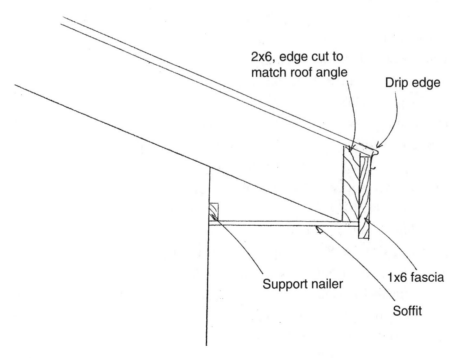

Soffit and eave detail.

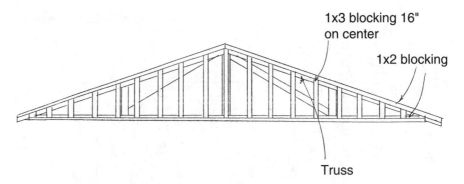

Truss-end blocking.

Materials List:

studs, precut: 125 req'd (more or less depending on quality of material)

end bottom plates: 2 × 4 in. × 12 ft., 4 req'd

side bottom plates: 2 × 4 in. × 16 ft., 4 req'd

end top plates: 2 × 4 in. × 12 ft., 4 req'd

side top plates: 2 × 4 in. × 16 ft., 4 req'd

end tie plates: 2 × 4 in. × 12 ft., 4 req'd

side tie plates: 2 × 4 in. × 16 ft., 4 req'd

wind bracing: 1 × 4 in. × 12 ft., 6 req'd

headers: 2 × 10 in. × 10 ft., 6 req'd

trusses, pre-engineered: 24 ft., 17 req'd

truss end supports: 2 × 6 in. × 16 ft., 4 req'd

truss bottom center support: 2 × 4 in. × 12 ft., 3 req'd

truss end blocking: 1 × 3 × 104 lineal ft. req'd

truss fastener blocks: 2 × 4 × 12 in., 34 req'd

siding, T 1–11: 4 × 8 ft. plywood, 34 sheets req'd

Z-flashing: 50 lineal ft. req'd

sheathing: CD 4 × 8 × ½ in. plywood, 32 req'd

gable rake board: 1 × 6 in. × 16 ft., cut to fit, 4 req'd

eave soffit, metal: 6 req'd

J-Channel: 6 req'd

eave fascia: 1 × 6 × 12 ft., 6 req'd

roofing felt, #15: 3 rolls req'd

drip edge: 120 lineal ft. req'd

shingles: 10 square req'd

corner trim: 1 × 4 in. × 8 ft., 8 req'd

door and window trim: 1 × 4 in. × 130 lineal ft. req'd (depending on number of doors and windows)

garage door facer trim: 1 × 6 in. × 10 ft., 2 req'd

garage door facer trim: 1 × 6 in. × 8 ft., 4 req'd

door: 36 in. pre-hung metal, 1 req'd

window: 32 × 36 in., single hung, 1 req'd

windows: 24 × 36 in., single hung, 2 req'd

garage doors, metal uninsulated: 7 × 9 ft., 2 req'd

garage door inside headers: 2 × 6 in. × 8 ft., 4 req'd

garage door inside headers: 2 × 6 in. × 10 ft., 2 req'd

caulk: 10 tubes req'd

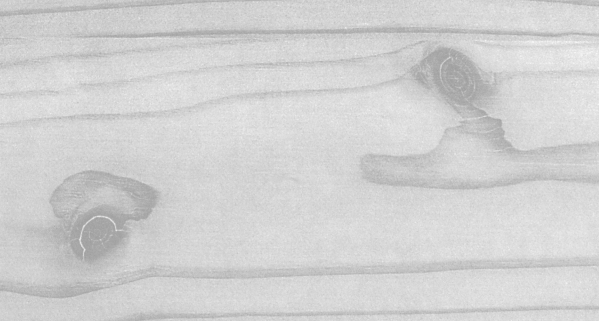

SECTION VIII

ANIMAL HOUSES AND FEEDERS

Many backyards and "mini-farms" provide shelter and a place to raise pets and other animals. These include chickens, small animals such as rabbits, even a pig, butcher calf, or a horse or two. Backyards are also great places for birdhouses and feeders. The projects in this section run from the smallest, simplest birdhouse to a one-stall horse barn.

CHAPTER 1

BIRDHOUSES

BUILDING AND ERECTING BIRDHOUSES
can lure many types of songbirds to your backyard. Most birdhouses are quite easy to build, but specific sizes, entrance
openings, and other factors must be met to attract specific
birds including wrens, bluebirds, robins, and martins.

BLUEBIRD HOUSES

Bluebird houses are some of the most popular birdhouses.
These colorful birds nest in natural cavities, but these days
they readily take to houses erected specially for them. A
house or two in your backyard can attract these useful insect
eaters. But be careful—wasps build their nests in the houses
and sparrows will quickly take them over. Construct them so
that they are easily cleaned of either of these unwanted
"house guests." Shown are two bluebird house designs. The
first utilizes a top that is removed by unscrewing one screw.
The second design utilizes a hinged door that allows you to
simply open the door and "sweep" out the debris. Either
house is very easy and fun to build.

The colorful bluebird will readily set up housekeeping in a custom-made home.

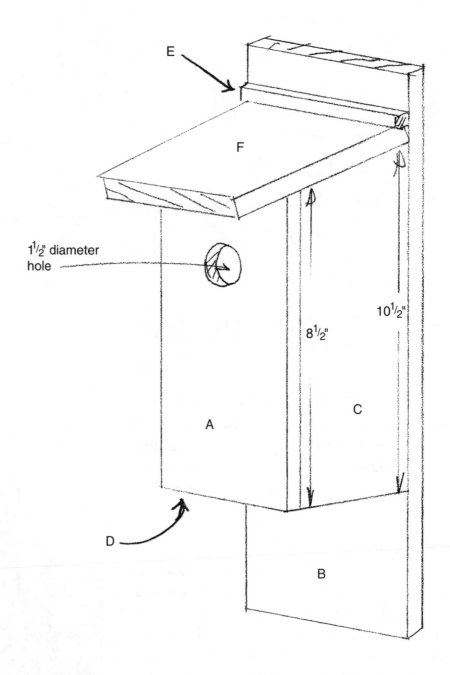

E

F

1½" diameter hole

10½"

8½"

C

A

D

B

BLUEBIRD HOUSE ONE

Cut the front and back to size. Locate and bore the 1½-inch diameter entry hole in the front. Then cut the sides including their angled tops. Fasten the front to the sides and then fasten the back to the sides. Cut the bottom to size and shape and then fasten it in place between the sides, front, and back. Cut the overhanging top piece. Rip a small strip for the top holding cleat. Insert the back edge of the top under the holding cleat and use an exterior screw down through the top and into the front to hold the top in place. To clean, merely unscrew the holding screw and slide the top back out of the way.

Materials List

A. front: ¾ × 5½ × 8½ in., 1 req'd

B. back: ¾ × 5½ × 16 in., 1 req'd

C. sides: ¾ × 4 × 10½ in., 2 req'd

D. bottom: ¾ × 4 × 4 in., 1 req'd

E. holding cleat: ¾ × ¾ × 5½ in., 1 req'd

F. top: ¾ × 5½ × 6½ in., 1 req'd

BLUEBIRD HOUSE TWO

The second house is constructed in much the same manner. Cut the pieces to the correct size and shapes. Bore the entry hole in the front. Fasten the back to the left-hand side piece. Place the front down on the left side and fasten it in place. Position the right side between the back and the front and mark its location, but do not anchor it in place. Mark the location of the bottom and top pieces on the right-hand side of the back. Then place the bottom in place and anchor it to the front, back and left-hand side. Place the top in position on the front and left-hand side and locate it correctly on the back according to the mark by the location of the back top of the right-hand side. Fasten the top in place with screws down through the top and into the front, left-hand side, and with screws through the back into the back edge of the top. Cut the top trim strip and fasten down on the top with screws from the back into the trim strip.

Fit the right-hand door in place. Drill a hole through the front and back near the top of the right-hand side. Make sure the holes are the same distance from the bottom of the right-hand side. Then drive a No. 4 galvanized nail into each of the holes. These act as pivoting hinges that allow the side to pivot out for easy cleaning. A screen-door hook or wooden thumb button is used to keep the door closed.

Materials List

A. back: ¾ × 5½ × 16 in., 1 req'd

B. sides: ¾ × 5½ × 11 in., 2 req'd

C. front: ¾ × 5½ × 10 in., 1 req'd

D. bottom: ¾ × 4 × 5½ in., 1 req'd

E. top: ¾ × 5½ × 8 in., 1 req'd

F. top trim: ¾ × ¾ × 5½ in., 1 req'd

G. thumb button: ¾ × ¾ × 1½ in., 1 req'd or screen-door hook, 1 req'd

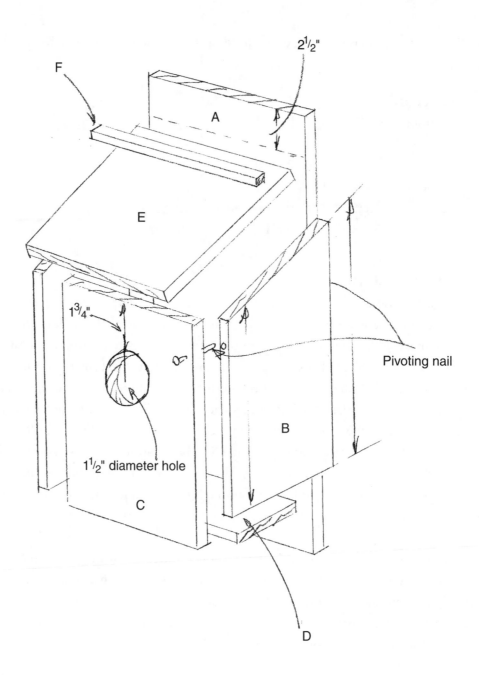

WREN HOUSE

Wrens are fun little birds. They'll build nests almost anywhere. One continued to build a nest under the seat of my old 8-N Ford tractor for many years. She simply followed the tractor to the field. Wrens are also very territorial. Build several nest houses and scatter them around your backyard to attract more then one wren. It doesn't take much in the way of materials or time to build this house. It's also one the kids will enjoy building with you.

Build more than one wren house to attract several of these charming birds to your yard.

The first step is to rip a piece of ½-inch treated plywood to 5½ inches wide. Cut off the long top piece. Then rip the remainder of the plywood to 5 inches. Cut the shorter top piece, the ends, and bottom to the correct length. Cut the "gables" on the ends. Locate and bore the hole in the front using an expansion or spade bit. Then cut the sides and bottom piece to the correct size. The top edges of the sides should be cut with the saw set at a 45-degree angle.

Fasten a side piece in place to both the front and back using No. 4 galvanized nails, or ¾-inch self-starting wood screws. Install the opposite side piece in the same manner. Fit the bottom in place and anchor it with screws or No. 4 galvanized nails. Fit the short top piece in place, with its top edge flush with the angled edges of the "gable" ends. Fit the opposite larger, top piece in place with its upper edge flush with the outer

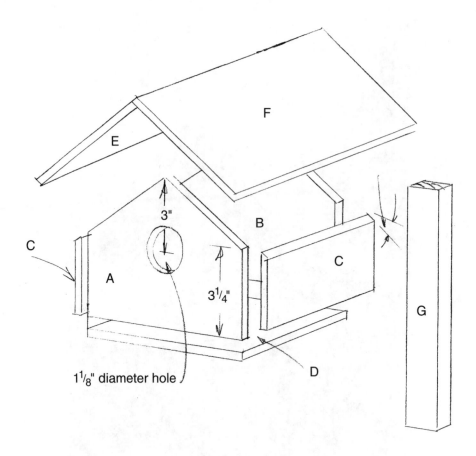

edge of the first installed top piece. The entire house can be assembled with screws or nails. I prefer to use screws, at least on the upper top piece. This allows me to remove the upper top piece in late winter for easy cleaning.

The house can be hung from a screw eye in the top of the roof. Or you can make a hanger strip from ¾-inch stock. Fasten the hanger strip in place with No. 6 galvanized nails. Fasten the house to a post or tree with screws through the hanger strip into the support.

Materials List
A. front: ½ in. plywood, 5 × 6 in., 1 req'd
B. back: ½ in. plywood, 5 × 6 in., 1 req'd
C. sides: ½ in. plywood, 3½ × 5 in., 2 req'd
D. bottom: ½ in. plywood, 4 × 5 in., 1 req'd
E. left top: ½ in. plywood, 5 × 6½ in., 1 req'd
F. right top: ½ in. plywood, 5½ × 6½ in., 1 req'd
G. hanger strip: ¾ × 1½ × 10 in., 1 req'd

MARTIN HOUSE

Martin houses are some of the most popular backyard birdhouses. An adult martin can eat its own weight in flying insects, or about two thousand mosquitoes a day. A colony of martins can wreck havoc on flying insects in your backyard. And, they're fun to watch as well. Because martins tend to nest in colonies, multiple-unit houses are a good idea. Most multiple-unit martin houses are designed with the rooms horizontal, or at the most two stories. Many are designed with solid, hard-to-clean construction. You literally have to dig the old nests, sparrow nests, and other debris out with a bent coat-hanger wire. The three-story "townhouse" I designed features a vertical rather than horizontal construction. It has two end doors on hinges with latches that provide easy access to all nests on both floors and both sides of the house. The house also has an attic stuffed with insulation to help keep heat down in hot temperatures.

The first step in construction is to cut the two ends to length. Then lay out and cut the upper angled "gable" ends. Lay out the entry holes and bore with a hole saw in a portable electric drill. Cut the bottom to size, and then fasten the two ends to the bottom with self-starting exterior wood screws. Cut the ceiling to size and fasten the ceiling between the two ends with wood screws. Cut the center divider to size and fit it between the bottom and ceiling. Make sure the divider is located exactly in the center of the box and then temporarily tack-nail it in place.

To create the compartment dividers, first cut the horizontal and vertical dividers to the correct width and length from ½-inch stock. Mark the locations of the "slots" in each divider using a small square. To make the cutouts, clamp the stock in a vise and cut on the lines using a fine-toothed hand saw. Then use a chisel to cut between the two and remove the slot. Or you can use a jigsaw or scroll saw to make these cutouts. Repeat the steps to create all the slots. Assemble one compartment side and slide it in position between the opposite house side and the interior divider. Then assemble the second compartment dividers and slide the assembly into position between the opposite house side and the interior divider. If everything fits properly, fasten the interior divider in place with screws through the bottom and ceiling. If anything needs to be adjusted, loosen the center divider and shift until everything fits properly, then anchor everything in place.

Cut the beveled side top pieces and fasten them in place to the ceiling and to the upper edges of the ends with wood screws. Rip the perches to the correct width, cut to length, and install in place with wood screws. Cut and install the right-hand side top in place, allowing it to protrude past each end 1½ inches. Cut the left-hand side top, but before you fasten it in place, stuff insulation in over top of the ceiling and between the

A martin house, built for multiple occupancy, is an attractive addition to the backyard.

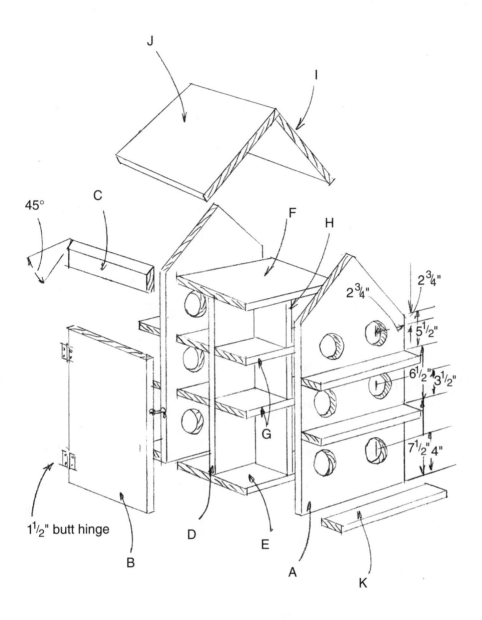

roof pieces, holding the insulation down with the unfastened roof piece. Then install the left-hand roof piece in place.

Cut the doors to the correct size and install to the ends with ½-inch butt hinges. Install screen-door hooks to hold the doors shut.

The biggest problem with martin houses is often erecting them. A simple metal strap can be used for either square or round poles. Martin houses should be erected 12 to 20 feet off the ground and in an open area with no large trees or buildings within 20 feet. They must also be taken down to clean each year. Although a ladder can be used, a cantilevered pole with a tilting upper portion makes the chore easier.

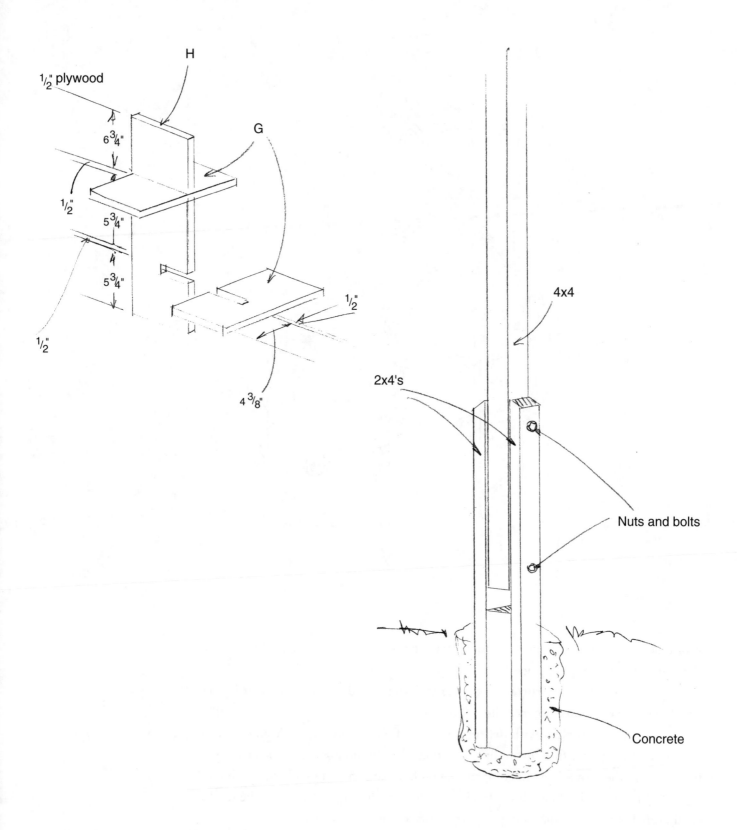

½" plywood

H

G

6¾"

½"

5¾"

5¾"

½"

4⅜"

½"

4x4

2x4's

Nuts and bolts

Concrete

Materials List

A. ends: ¾ × 11½ × 25¾ in., 2 req'd

B. side doors: ¾ × 11½ × 18 in., 2 req'd

C. upper sides: ¾ × 1½ × 11½ in., 2 req'd

D. inside divider: ¾ × 11½ × 18 in., 1 req'd

E. bottom: ¾ × 10 × 11½ in., 1 req'd

F. ceiling: ¾ × 10 × 11½ in., 1 req'd

G. horizontal compartment dividers: ½ × 4¾ × 11½ in., 4 req'd

H. vertical compartment dividers: ½ × 4¾ × 18 in., 2 req'd

I. right-side roof: ¾ × 10¾ × 14½ in., 1 req'd

J. left-side roof: ¾ × 11½ × 14½ in., 1 req'd

K. outside perches: ¾ × 1¾ × 11½ in., 6 req'd

L. butt hinges: 1 in., 2 pair req'd

M. screen door hooks: 2 req'd

N. galvanized nails: No. 6 × 1¼ in. and No. 6 × 2½ in.

CHAPTER 2

BIRD FEEDERS

BIRD FEEDERS ARE ALSO FUN and easy to build. They make great projects for youngsters, and feeders can be used to attract many bird species to your backyard.

Shown are three different designs: a suspended or pole type feeder, a window feeder, and a platform feeder for ground feeding birds.

SUSPENDED BIRD FEEDER

This feeder can be suspended from a tree with a rope or fastened to a pole. In either case, use metal squirrel baffles to prevent squirrels from raiding it. The feeder is fairly large. It will hold about a gallon and a half of feed at a time. It's also divided so that you can provide two separate types of feed.

The first step is to cut the hopper bottom to the correct size and shape. Then cut the interior divider to size and shape. Fasten the hopper bottom down over the interior divider with wood screws. Cut the sides to shape, making sure their angles are correct. Fasten the sides to the hopper bottom as well as the interior divider, making sure the latter is square and located in the center of the ends. Then fasten the top piece in place down over the ends and the interior divider. Cut the Plexiglas hopper sides to shape using a band saw or fine-toothed hand saw. Fasten in place to the angled sides with flat-head brass screws. Note, you will have to pre-drill the holes with a ⅛-inch bit to prevent splitting out the Plexiglas.

Cut the roof pieces. Note the upper edges are cut at a 45-degree angle. Fasten the roof pieces to the center top piece with 1-inch butt hinges.

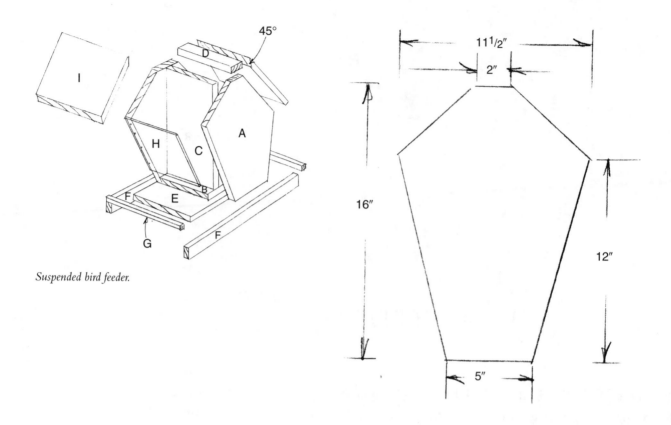

Suspended bird feeder.

Create the feeding platform and perches by first cutting the platform bottom to size and shape. Cut the bottom side strips to size and shape and fasten to the bottom, keeping their bottom edges flush with the platform bottom. Cut and fasten the perches in place. Note, you will also have to pre-drill these to prevent splitting out the narrow stock.

Turn the hopper upside down and place the feed platform down over it. Note the feed platform fits inside the bottom sidepieces. Fasten in place with wood screws through the feed platform bottom and bottom sidepieces into the hopper bottom.

To hang the house, use a screw eye in the top. To install on a post top, you can use metal L-brackets, screwing into the feed platform bottom and the post.

Materials List
A. sides: ¾ × 11½ × 16 in., 2 req'd
B. hopper bottom: ¾ × 5 × 7 in., 1 req'd
C. divider: ¾ × 7 × 15¼ in., 1 req'd
D. top: ¾ × 2 × 8½ in., 1 req'd
E. feeder bottom: ¾ × 8½ × 15 in., 1 req'd
F. feeder side edges: ¾ × 1½ × 18 in., 2 req'd
G. feeder end edges: ¾ × ¾ × 8½ in., 2 req'd

H. Plexiglas: 8½ × 10½ in., 2 req'd

I. feeder lids: ¾ × 8½ × 8½ in., 2 req'd

WINDOW FEEDER

A house window bird feeder allows close-up watching of your favorite feathered friends. The feeder is designed to be fastened to the bottom window trim. It's extremely easy to make and install. Because it fits against the window, it doesn't have a back. First step is to cut the bottom to the correct size and shape. Then cut the sides to size and shape. Fasten the sides to the bottom with screws driven through the bottom into the lower ends of the sides with wood screws. Cut the Plexiglas front piece and fasten it in place with brass flat-head wood screws. You will have to pre-drill the holes with a ⅛-inch drill bit to prevent splitting out the Plexiglas. Cut the solid top piece and anchor it to the back of the sides with screws. Then cut the lift-up top lid to size and anchor it in place with butt hinges fastened to the solid top piece. The house is held in place on the windowsill with an anchoring strip on the bottom. Determine your particular window trim and house location, and then fasten the anchor strip in the correct location on the underside of the feeder bottom. Finally, fasten the anchor strip to the window sill. This should position the feeder fairly close to the window. You can move the anchor strip in or out as needed.

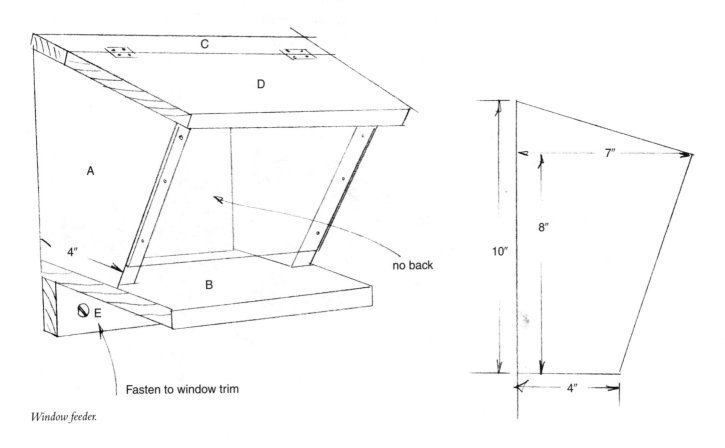

Window feeder.

Materials List

A. sides: ¾ × 7½ × 10 in., 2 req'd

B. bottom: ¾ × 8 × 12 in., 1 req'd

C. top: ¾ × 1½ × 12 in., 1 req'd

D. lid: ¾ × 7 × 12 in., 1 req'd

E. fastening strip: ¾ × 1½ × 12 in., 1 req'd

F. Plexiglas: 6½ × 12 in., 1 req'd

PLATFORM FEEDER

This is one of the easiest feeders to build, and will be well appreciated by ground feeding birds, such as juncos, field sparrows, chickadees, quail, and others. It consists of a wooden platform with a bottom of ¼-inch exterior plywood, or ⅜-inch treated materials. A ¾-×-1½-inch wooden apron around the sides prevents seeds from being scattered to the four winds. If you need to keep squirrels out of it, simply add a section of ½-inch hardware cloth over the top. This allows birds to peck through the hardware cloth, but squirrels can't dig the feed out.

Materials List

A. bottom: ¼-in exterior plywood, 24 × 24 in., 1 req'd

B. skirting: ¾ × 1½ × 24 in., 2 req'd

C. skirting: ¾ × 1½ × × 22½ in., 2 req'd

D. hardware cloth: ½ in., 24 × 24 in., req'd

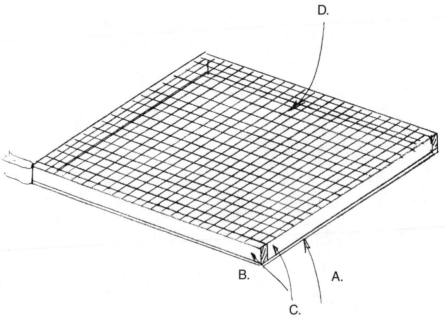

Platform feeder.

CHAPTER 3

POULTRY HOUSING

RAISING CHICKENS IN YOUR backyard is a great way of getting some homegrown, organic meat, as well as eggs. Chickens are the most popular homesteader critters. Chickens can also be fun, especially with youngsters. Chickens do require some special housing needs, starting when they are young and through raising them to fryers, or as laying flocks. Over the years, many types of buildings have been designed to raise and/or house chickens. The building shown is one of the most versatile, allowing you to use it to raise baby chicks, grow them to fryers, or keep a flock of layers. One of the main attributes is the house is on skids and portable. A large, front yard is enclosed. This protects the birds from predators and keeps them contained when you desire to keep them in one location. The skids also mean you can move the unit around your pasture or large back lot to keep the birds on "clean" ground in the front enclosure. The building proper, which also sits on the skids, has a wooden floor. This prevents predators from getting to the birds locked inside, and keeps them up off the ground during the night or inclement weather. The house features standard frame construction, clapboard or plywood siding, a sheathed roof covered with shingles for insulation and protection, and tilt-down windows in the front to allow for ventilation—a very important factor in successfully raising poultry.

The first step in construction is to cut the angled ends on the skids and fasten the three 4-×-4 cross braces between the skids with lag screws. Then fasten floor joists between the skids. Install a ¾-inch treated plywood floor over the floor joists on the rear portion of the two skids. Frame-in the building using standard wood frame methods,

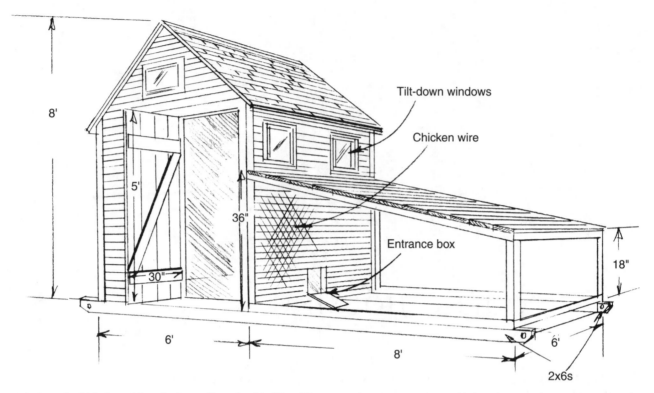

8'

Tilt-down windows

Chicken wire

5'

36"

Entrance box

30"

18"

6'

8'

6'

2x6s

Chickens should be housed in a dry, but well ventilated building. The version shown is not only portable but also versatile, suitable as a brooder, grower, or laying house.

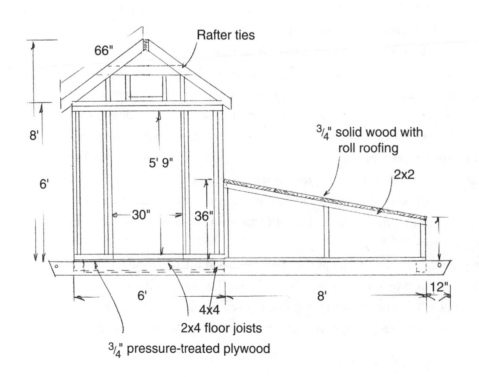

Rafter ties

66"

3/4" solid wood with roll roofing

8'

5' 9"

2x2

6'

30"

36"

6'

8'

12"

4x4

2x4 floor joists

3/4" pressure-treated plywood

stand up the sides on the wood floor, and anchor the sides together. Cut and fasten the rafters in place. Add the siding, roof sheathing, and shingles. Then build the doors and/or windows and install in place. Note the entrance box drop-down ramp is hinged at the bottom and uses a string latch from the inside to fasten it up in place.

The next step is to construct the outer framework for the enclosed yard. The outer ends use 4-×-4 posts. These are held in place with metal straps and L-brackets. Fasten 2-×-4 upright supports to the building edges for the rear supports. A 2 × 6, 8-foot long, is fastened on either side at the top and a 2 × 4 at the bottom for the sides. A 2 × 4 at the top and bottom on the end provides support there. Then add ½-inch treated plywood as a top, covering with roll roofing, or you can use ¾-inch white cedar boards for the yard covering. Finally, fasten ½-inch hardware cloth around the two sides and the end.

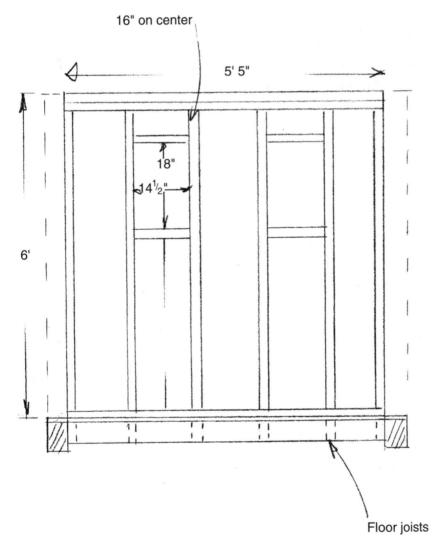

16" on center

5' 5"

18"

14½"

6'

Floor joists

Side view.

Materials List

skids, pressure treated: 4 × 6 in. × 16 ft. 2 req'd

cross braces: 4 × 4 in. × 6 ft. cut to fit, 3 req'd

studs: 2 × 4 in. precut, 35 req'd

rafters: 2 × 4 × 72 in., cut to fit, 8 req'd

ridge board: 2 × 4 in. × 7 ft., 1 req'd

rafter ties: 2 × 4 × 48 in., 6 req'd

floor: ¾-in. plywood, 4 × 8 ft. 2 sheets, cut to fit

floor joists: 2 × 4 in. × 6 ft. cut to fit, 6 req'd

door: ¾-in. plywood, or plank 1 × 12s, 30 in. × 5 ft. 9 in.

...near feet req'd

...ng: ½-in. plywood sheathing, 4 × 8 ft., 3 req'd

roofing, composite: ⅔ square req'd

yard framing: 2 × 2 in., 70 linear feet req'd

netting: ½-in. hardware cloth, 36 in. wide, 1 roll req'd

yard covering: ¾-in. solid sheathing, 1 × 12 in. × 6 ft. 9 req'd

roll roofing: 1 roll req'd

CHAPTER 4

RABBIT HOUSING

RABBITS ARE FUN TO RAISE. They can provide nutritious meat that is lower in fat and higher in minerals than many other types of meat. Rabbits also supply soft, beautiful, and easily tanned furs or skins. Rabbits can be raised in cages in buildings, but the simplest and most economical shelter is an outside hutch. This is basically a cage with a back and top. The sides and front are left open for ventilation and are covered with hardware cloth. Detachable wind protectors, held in place with wing nuts, are made for the sides to provide protection from cold winter winds. The bottom is also hardware cloth to allow for droppings to fall through. Rabbits tend to chew on wood, so the hardware cloth covering must be stapled to the inside. This area, however, tends to collect urine and odor. One solution I've seen is metal flashing cut into strips and fastened down over the wire. This allows for easier "hosing" out of the cages and leaves less odor. The top, back, and removable side panels are all made of ½-inch pressure-treated plywood. The top can be further protected with roll roofing, stapled in place, and the staples covered with roofing asphalt. The entire framework is constructed of 2 × 2s. These should also be made of pressure-treated materials, ripping them to the correct size from 2 × 4s.

First step in construction is to rip the 2 × 4s and construct the end frames. Fasten together with two self-starting brass wood screws at each joint. Make sure the frames are constructed square. Then strengthen with metal T-brackets, fastening in place with brass screws. Construct the bottom framework in the same fashion. Use

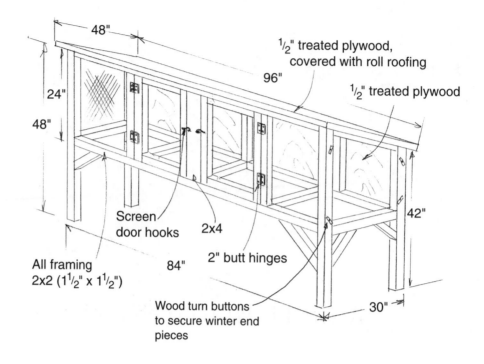

T- or L-brackets on the bottom of the joints for further strength. Construct the top framework. Fasten the bottom framework in place to the end frames, again using screws and T-fasteners at the joints. Make sure the structure is sitting on a flat, smooth, and level surface. Square up the frames and install the diagonal bracing on the front and back. Then install the top frame. Cut the uprights for the back and install between the bottom and top frame. Cut the uprights for the front and install them as well. Cut and install the hardware cloth on the bottom, ends, and front, using staples. Then cut and install the plywood back. Finally, fasten the top in place and apply the roofing material.

Cut the doorframes and assembly the doors. Cover the doors on the inside with hardware cloth, then hinge in place. Wooden turn-buttons are used to hold the doors closed, or you can use screen door hooks.

Materials List

front legs: 2 × 2 × 48 in., 2 req'd

rear legs: 2 × 2 × 42 in., 2 req'd

lower side braces: 2 × 2 × 27 in., 2 req'd

upper side braces: 2 × 2 × 28 in. (cut to fit), 2 req'd

front and back, bottom and top braces: 2 × 2 × 81 in., 4 req'd

bottom front to back center braces: 2 × 2 × 27 in., 3 req'd

top front to back center braces: 2 × 2 × 28 in., 3 req'd

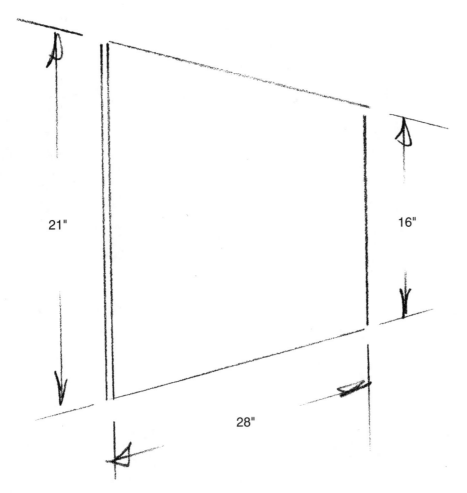

Winter end panels.

front uprights: 2 × 2 × 21 in., 2 req'd
center front upright: 2 × 4 × 21 in., 1 req'd
rear uprights: 2 × 2 × 15 in., 3 req'd
door uprights: 2 × 2 × 21 in., 4 req'd
door horizontals: 2 × 2 × 20 in., 4 req'd
top: ½ in.-×-4 ×-8-ft. treated plywood, 1 req'd
winter end panels: ½-in. treated plywood, 21 × 28 in., 2 req'd
butt hinges: 2 in., 4 req'd
½-in. hardware cloth: 30 in. wide roll, 1 req'd
½-in. staples
T-brackets: 20 req'd
strap brackets: 6 req'd

SMALL ANIMAL SHELTER

GOATS, SHEEP, PIGS, a beef calf, even llamas and emus should have some type of shelter from inclement weather, as well as shade from the heat of the day and the sun. The shed shown is an extremely simple and economical pole-shelter. It can be covered with rough-sawn, green lumber, which was often a choice years ago, or it can be sided with wood or corrugated metal. The poles and bottom supports are all pressure-treated woods for long life. The front of the shed is extremely versatile, and can be constructed to suit the animal or use needed. The front can be completely enclosed with a standard entry door, enclosed at the bottom with a lower gate or door, or partially enclosed with a gate or door. The front can also be left completely open for shelter in a pasture, or it can be used with a pen in front to contain the animals.

Construction is standard pole-style and very easy to do. Lay out the outline of the building and mark the pole locations. Make sure the building is laid out square. Using a power or hand post-hole digger, dig the holes for the posts. Position the posts in place in the holes. Plumb and brace the poles in place. Temporarily fasten a skirting board around the bottom and check with a carpenter's square to assure the poles are correctly located to create a square building. Reposition posts and reset the skirting as needed. Once all posts are positioned correctly, pour concrete around them and allow it to set for a couple of days. Then anchor the lower skirting or "girts" solidly in place. Install the middle and upper girts to the poles. Cut the 2-×-6 rafters to the correct length and angles and fasten them in place on top of the upper girts. Then cut the 2-×-4 purlins to correct length and fasten them down on the rafters.

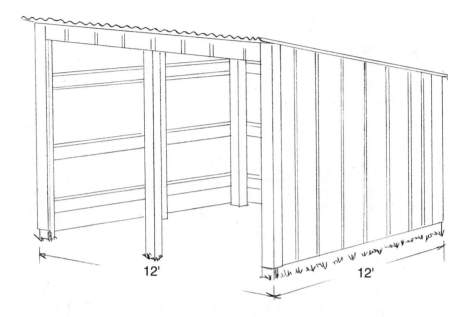

Install the corrugated metal or plastic roofing down on the purlins. Frame-in the doors or openings, and then install the siding to three or all sides of the building. Metal corner trim can be used to finish off and cover the cut edges of the metal siding. Wood blocking is used on the front of the posts to fasten the corner trim in place.

Materials List

posts: 4 × 4 in. × 10 ft., 5 req'd
posts: 4 × 4 in. × 8 ft., 3 req'd

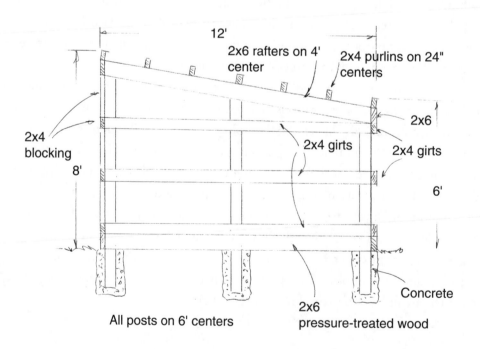

girts: 2 × 4 in. × 12 ft., 3 req'd

girts: 2 × 4 in. × 11 ft. 9 in., 6 req'd

rafters: 2 × 6 in. × 12 ft., 4 req'd

purlins: 2 × 4 in. × 12 ft., 7 req'd

front and back fascia: 2 × 6 in. × 12 ft., 2 req'd

skirting: 2 × 6 in. × 12 ft., 3 req'd

metal siding: laps to 36 in. × 8 ft., 12 req'd

metal corner trim: 8 ft., 8 req'd

metal roofing: lap to 36 in. × 14 ft., 4 req'd

blocking: 2 × 4 in. × 8 ft. cut to fit, 3 req'd

concrete

ONE-STALL HORSE STABLE

IN MOST INSTANCES, HORSES should have some sort of shelter. The one-horse stable shown not only has a roomy, airy, 10-×-12 foot box stall, but a 4-×-10 foot, built-in tack/feed room on one end that keeps everything handy in one spot. The shelter is also on skids. You can simply move it around the pasture or lot, for easy cleanup and fewer fly and insect problems. The skids are made of pressure-treated materials for long life. A double, Dutch-style front door provides entry and cross ventilation when needed. Metal roofing provides an economical protection. A center section utilizes translucent panels for more light.

The first step in construction begins by cutting the ends of the 4-×-6 pressure-treated side skids to an angle. Then bore holes in their ends so cable can be anchored to pull the stable around. Fasten the three 4-×-4 supports between the front and back 4-×-6 skids with lag screws and then fasten the 2-×-4 floor joists for the inside divider wall between the front and back 4 × 6s. Use lag screws for all joints. Then add the 2-×-4 cross floor joists. Do all this assembly on a smooth, flat, level surface.

Cut the ¾-inch treated plywood floor to size and install on the storage room joists. Next frame up the front wall, noting it must have two bottom plates, one to fit over the ¾-inch floor of the storage room and one for the stall. The simplest method is to frame the storage room and stall separately, and join the two to create a single wall. Brace the front wall sections solidly in place, making sure they are plumb and then use a second top plate to join them together. Frame up the rear wall in the same manner and then frame the two end walls and install them between the front and back walls.

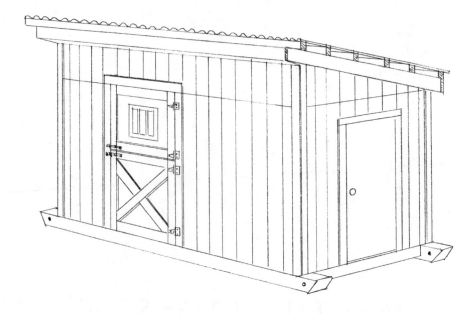

The end walls have an angled single top plate with vertical blocking supporting them. Again, make sure they are plumb. Note the storage end wall must be ¾ inch shorter than the stall end wall. Frame up and install the inner divider wall for the storage room and then install the top plates to tie all the walls together.

Install the siding, cutting the openings for the windows. Z-flashing is used at the top of the 8-foot siding sheets. The upper portions of the side and front are then sided. Siding is also installed on the interior divider wall, on the inside of the storage shed

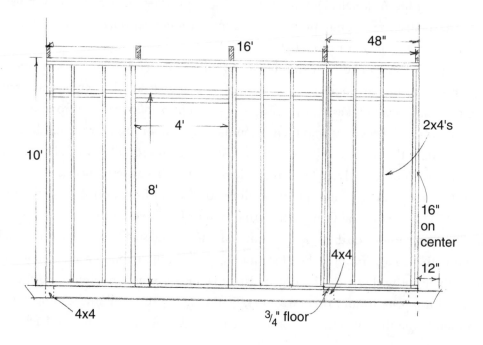

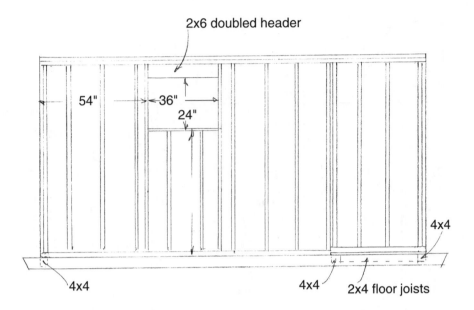

portion. Note, you may wish to add ¾-inch kickboards up about 4 feet on the inside of the stall area. Windows with screens may be installed, but metal window guards should be installed on the inside. An alternative is to create "open" windows with shutters that may be closed in cold or inclement weather. The stable door is 4 feet wide for easy entry and consists of top and bottom halves. The upper and bottom sections are constructed utilizing plywood with 2-×-2 backing and 1-×-4 treated front boards. Sturdy hinges and latches are installed. The upper door also has a steel-guarded opening. The tack-room door is a standard steel, pre-framed 36-inch door.

The roof framing is pole-barn style with five 2-×-6 rafters spaced 4 feet apart. Their ends are cut to the correct angles and they are installed on top of the wall plates using Strong-Tie H1 Seismic and Hurricane Anchors or blocking to anchor the rafters upright. Next, install 1 × 6 fascia boards over the ends of the rafters. Then fasten 2-×-4 purlins, spaced 24-inches apart, over the rafters. Corrugated aluminum, steel, or reinforced fiberglass/plastic panels are then installed over the purlins. A center section of translucent materials allows for light.

Materials List

skids: 4 × 6 in. × 18 ft., 2 req'd

end and storage wall supports: 4 × 4 in. × 10 ft., 3 req'd

studs: 2-×-4 in. precuts, 60 req'd

studs: 2 × 4 in. × 10 ft., 19 req'd

front and back plates: 2 × 4 in. × 16 ft., 6 req'd

end plates: 2 × 4 in. × 10 ft., 6 req'd

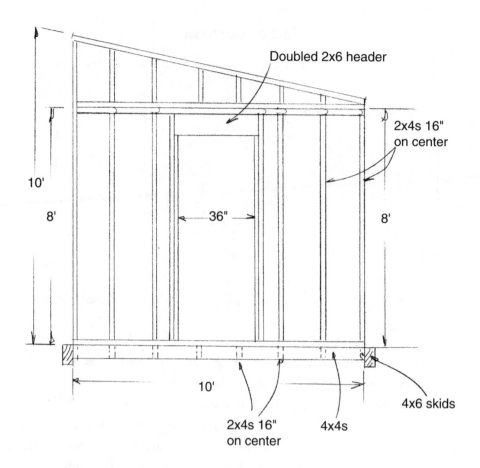

storage wall plates: 2 × 4 in. × 10 ft., 3 req'd

angled end plate: 2 × 4 in. × 12 ft., cut to fit, 2 req'd

headers: 2 × 6 in. × 14 ft., cut to fit, 1 req'd

storage room floor: ¾-in. plywood × 4 × 10 ft., 1 req'd

storage room floor joists: 2 × 4 in. × 4 ft., cut to fit, 8 req'd

siding: 4 × 8 ft. plywood, 18 req'd

rafters: 2 × 6 in. × 12 ft., 5 req'd

purlins: 2 × 4 in. × 18 ft., 6 req'd

fascia boards: 1 × 8 in. × 16 ft., 2 req'd

roofing, corrugated translucent: 12 ft., 1 sheet req'd

roofing, corrugated metal: 12 ft., cut to fit, 5 sheets req'd

door and window trim: 1 × 3 in., 150 linear feet req'd

pre-hung steel panel door: 36 ft., 1 req'd

window: 24 × 36 in., 3-panel sliding, 1 req'd

Z-flashing: 52 ft. req'd

hardware, hinges, metal door, and window grates

SOURCES

MANUFACTURERS:

Black & Decker
800–54-HOW-TO
www.BlackandDecker.com

Bon Tool Company
724–443–7080
www.bontool.com

Bosch Power Tools
877-BOSCH-99
www.boschtools.com

California Redwood Association
415–382–0662
www.calredwood.org

Campbell-Hausfeld
866-CHTools
www.chtools.com

Sears Craftsman Tools
800–377–7414
www.sears.com/craftsman

Cultured Stone Corp.
800–255–1727
www.culturedstone.com

Delta Machinery
800–428–2486
www.deltawoodworking.com

DeWalt
800–4-DEWALT
www.dewalt.com

Dremel
800–437–3635
www.dremel.com

Grizzly Industria
800–523–4777
www.grizzly.com

Hitachi Koki U.S.A., Ltd.
www.hitachi-koki.com

Louisiana-Pacific Corp.
800–648–6893
www.lpcorp.com

Makita U.S.A., Inc.
800–4MAKITA
www.makitatools.com

Marshalltown Trowel Company
800–888–0127
www.marshalltown.com

Milwaukee Electric Tool Corp.
877–729–3878
www.milwaukeetool.com

Porter–Cable
888–848–5175
www.porter-cable.com

QUIKRETE
800–282–5828
www.quikrete.com

Ryobi Technologies
800–525–2579
www.ryobitools.com

Simpson Strong-Tie Connectors
800–999–5099
www.strongtie.com

Skil Power Tools
877-SKIL-999
www.skiltools.com

The Stanley Works
800-STANLEY
www.stanleyworks.com

Suntuf, Inc.
800–999–9459
www.suntuf.com

Swing-N-Slide
800–888–1232
www.swing-n-slide.com

TimberKing
800–942–4406
www.timberking.com

Vaughan & Bushnell Mfg.
815–648–2446
www.vaughanmfg.com

Western Red Cedar Lumber Assoc.
866–778–9096
www.wrcla.org

Weyerhaeuser ChoiceDek
800–951–5117
www.choicedek.com

Wolmanized Natural Select wood
866–789–4567
www.naturalselect.com

Woodcraft Supply
800–225–1153
www.woodcraft.com

INDEX